Learning to Program

in

Pascal and Delphi

S. Langfield

B.Sc. (Hons)

Published by

Payne-Gallway Publishers Ltd

26-28 Northgate Street, Ipswich IP1 3DB

Tel: 01473 251097   Fax: 01473 232758

www.payne-gallway.co.uk

2003

Acknowledgements

I would like to thank my husband John for his support in the home while I spent many hours in my study writing this book. Thanks also to Alan Stinchcombe for proofreading and making valuable comments on many aspects of the text, which have resulted in a better book.

I am grateful to the Assessment and Qualifications Alliance (AQA) for permission to use questions from the 2003 Unit 3 (CPT3) examination paper, and to Alison Day for giving me feedback on the model answers to these questions.

Cover picture © 'Pram' reproduced with the kind permission of Robert McAulay

Cover photography © Mike Kwasniak, 160 Sidegate Lane, Ipswich

Cover design © Direction Advertising & Design Ltd

First edition 2003

10 9 8 7 6 5 4 3 2 1

A catalogue entry for this book is available from the British Library.

ISBN 1 904467 29 6

Copyright © S. Langfield 2003

Printed in Great Britain by

W M Print Ltd, Walsall, West Midlands

Preface

The aim of this book is to provide an introduction to programming in an imperative high-level language as required by the AQA AS Computing specification.

The book is divided into 3 sections covering introductions to Pascal, Delphi and the AQA CPT3 Practical Exercise.

The first two sections can either be used sequentially or in parallel. The **Pascal** section is essential as it gives students without any prior programming experience the opportunity to learn how to use the fundamental constructs of a high-level programming language. The **Delphi** section revisits these constructs and applies them in the context of the graphical user interface with its components, properties, methods and event-driven programming. For example, after completing chapter 3, chapter 12 could be covered, after chapter 4, chapter 13 could be covered, and so on.

The third section includes model solutions to the AQA 2003 **Practical Exercise**. These solutions have been produced using the programming techniques demonstrated in this book. They may not be the most elegant solutions possible, but they aim to show that the practical exercise can be solved with appropriate application of the fundamental constructs covered in this book.

Model answers to the programming exercises are available, to teachers only, from our website **www.payne-gallway.co.uk**

The intended audience

This book was written primarily for AS Computing students following the AQA specification. It will also be suitable for anyone wanting to learn to program in Pascal. The book also gives an introduction to the visual development tool Delphi and some of the many components available to produce event-driven applications.

Version of Delphi

This book was written using Borland Delphi 7. However, most of the components covered are also available in earlier versions of Delphi, and likely to be available in later versions.

Pascal is available in many different versions. The code editor interface may look slightly unfamiliar in different versions. The exercises can be written in any version of Pascal. Delphi 6 onwards has the Console Application feature that makes it very straight-forward to learn Pascal in the same software environment as that used to develop event-driven programs with graphical user interfaces, which students often enjoy working in much more.

A very useful web site for inspiration on Delphi programming, tutorials and example programs is **www.delphi.about.com**

For further reading, try 'Discover Delphi' by Shirley Williams and Sue Walmsley.

For those who would like to get much more involved with Delphi programming I recommend 'Mastering Delphi 6' by Marco Cantù.

Contents

Table of Contents

Part 1

Learning to Program in Pascal

In this section:

Chapter 1 – Introduction to Pascal

Pascal is an imperative, high-level programming language. It was designed as a general-purpose language in the late 1960s, long before graphical user interfaces were in common use. It was further developed into Object Pascal (an object-oriented programming language). Delphi is a visual programming tool using Object Pascal as its programming language. We can use Delphi to write simple Pascal programs known as console applications. These do not have a graphical user interface.

A Delphi Console Application

Delphi 7 has an Integrated Development Environment (IDE) enabling you to write programs with a Graphical User Interface (GUI). However, it is important that you understand the fundamental programming constructs first and the purpose of this section is to give you this understanding by practising your programming skills.

- Launch Delphi by selecting it from the **Start** menu. You will be presented with the IDE. However, we are going to learn about the programming constructs by writing Pascal code as a Console Application.

- Choose **File, New, Other**.

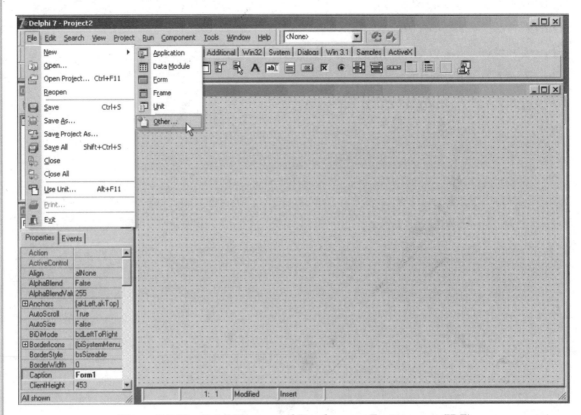

Figure 1.1: The Delphi Integrated Development Environment (IDE)

- Select the **Console Application** icon in the **New Items** window:

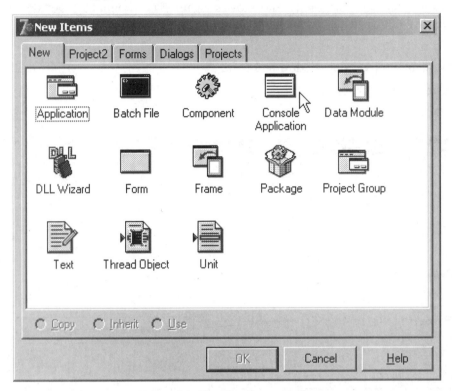

Figure 1.2: The New Items window

Delphi presents you with the outline of the program code you need for every console application:

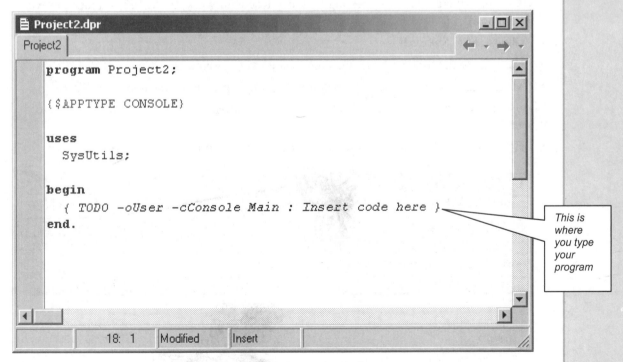

Figure 1.3: A new project code window

Note that you can run this program. Try it by clicking on the **Run** button. You may notice a black window opening very briefly and closing again. The program is not doing anything because we have not written any statements yet.

- Maximise the Project2.dpr window and write

    ```
    Writeln ('Hello World')
    ```

    as shown below:

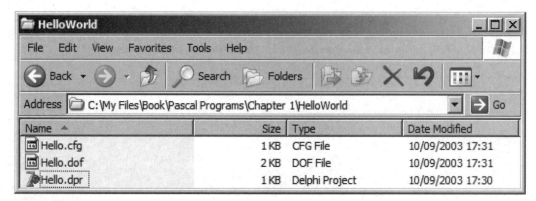

Figure 1.4: Writing the first line of code

Saving a program

If your program crashes during testing you may lose your work, so it is a good idea to save your program now.

- Choose **File, Save All**.

- Navigate to the folder where you want to store your programs.

- Make a new folder just for this program, or project, giving it the name *HelloWorld*.

Choosing a sensible file name, helps you to find your program when you want to return to it later.

- Have a look into the folder to see what Delphi has saved for this one small program:

Figure 1.5: The files created for one console application

- Now run this program.

  What happens?

  You might see a quick flash of a black window on the screen. Your program ran but when finished, the console window closed.

- To keep it open add the line

  ```
  Readln
  ```

- Run the program again. You should now see this window:

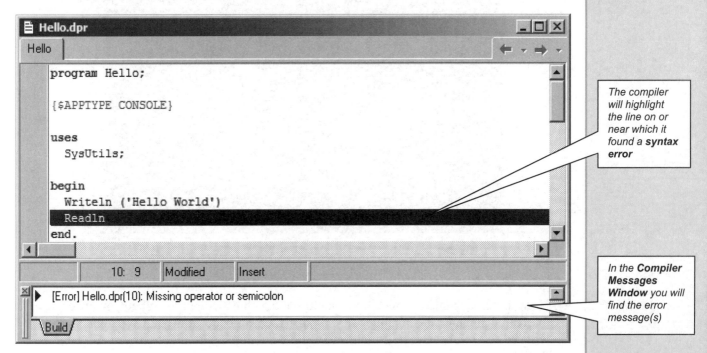

Figure 1.6: A compilation error

To separate this statement from the previous one you must use a semicolon (;).

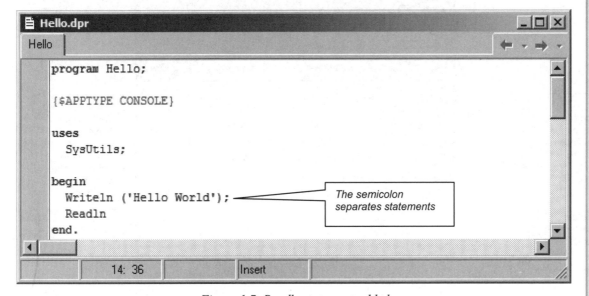

Figure 1.7: Readln statement added

The `Readln` statement waits for the user to press the **Enter** key, and therefore the console window will stay open until you press the **Enter** key.

- Run the program again.

You should see the following screen:

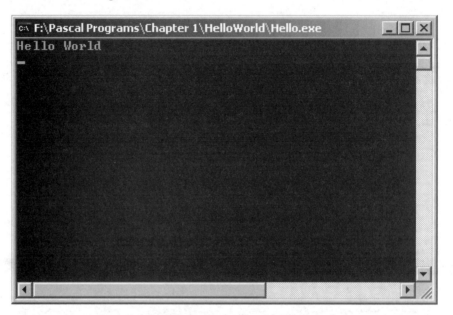

Figure 1.8: A Console Application Run window

- Now check your folder again. You should see the object code file. When you choose the **Run** command, the compiler first produces object code from your program. This is saved and can be executed again and again without recompiling, until you edit your Pascal program. Then it needs to be recompiled.

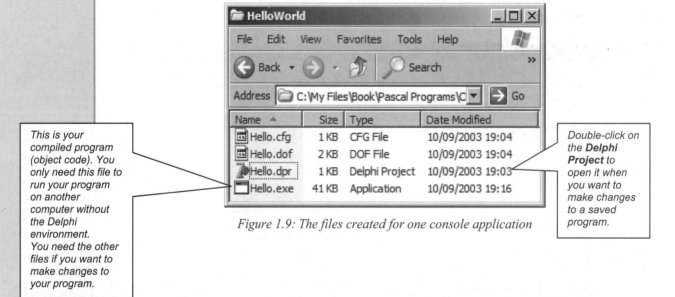

This is your compiled program (object code). You only need this file to run your program on another computer without the Delphi environment. You need the other files if you want to make changes to your program.

*Double-click on the **Delphi Project** to open it when you want to make changes to a saved program.*

Figure 1.9: The files created for one console application

Summary

You have learnt how to:
- ✓ start a console application
- ✓ produce a message in the Run window by using the `Writeln` statement
- ✓ keep the Run window open by using the `Readln` statement
- ✓ separate statements using a semicolon (;)
- ✓ save a console application using the **Save All** menu option
- ✓ load a previously saved console application by double-clicking on the **Delphi Project** file

Exercises

1.1 Write a program that will output two messages of your choice on the screen, on separate lines.

1.2 Write a program that will output this rocket on the screen:

```
         *
        * * *
       * * * * *
      * * * * * *
      * * * * * *
      * * * * * *
      * * * * * *
      * * * * * *
      * * * * * *
      * * * * * *
      * * * * * *
        * * *
       * * * * *
```

Chapter 2 – Input, Assignment and Output

Programs usually operate on data, to produce results.

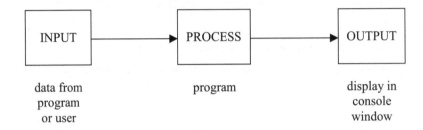

INPUT		PROCESS		OUTPUT
data from program or user		program		display in console window

Data may be supplied by the program code, but frequently the user enters data while the program is running. In Chapter 10 we will learn how to read data from files and save to files.

Variables

Let's look at a very simple program that adds two numbers and displays the sum. Any data the program uses needs to be stored in variables. You can think of these variables as labelled boxes that can each hold one data item:

Number1 ☐

Number2 ☐

Sum ☐

In reality, the 'boxes' are locations in the computer's main memory.

We call the box labels **identifiers**. As the programmer you must choose an appropriate identifier for each variable you use in your program. A valid identifier must start with a letter and can consist of any combination of letters, numerals and the underscore character (_), but not spaces.

For ease of understanding by other programmers, or yourself later on, your program should be self-explanatory or **self-documenting**.

To this end, choose an identifier that explains the purpose of your variable. For example, choose `NumberOfEntries` rather than `n5` or `number`.

Pascal is not case-sensitive, so that `Number`, `number`, `nUMBER`, `NUMBER` are all equivalent. However, this book uses the convention of 'CamelCaps' for ease of reading identifiers such as `NumberOfEntries`, without the need for underscores.

Pascal requires you to declare what type of data you are going to store in your chosen variables. Therefore if we want to store whole numbers we need to declare them as integers at the beginning of our program code in the **var** section:

Figure 2.1: Declaring variables in a console application

The Assignment Statement

To store a value in a variable we use an assignment statement. For example, the following statement assigns the value 5 to the variable `Number1`:

```
Number1 := 5;
```

The `:=` is the assignment operator and the value on the right of the assignment operator is stored in the variable whose identifier is on the left of the assignment operator. It can be read as "becomes equal to" or "takes the value".

An assignment statement can also contain an expression on the right side of the assignment operator `:=`, which will be evaluated when that statement is executed.

```
Number1 := 5;
Number2 := 29;
Sum := Number1 + Number2;
```

The above statements will result in putting the value 34 into the variable `Sum`.

The Writeln Statement

When we want to display the content of a variable, we use the `Writeln` statement and provide the variable identifier in brackets:

```
Writeln (Number1)
```

Note the difference between displaying a message of the programmer's choice:

```
Writeln ('Number1');
```

and   `Writeln (Number1);`

which displays whatever value is contained in the variable `Number1`.

We can combine several variable identifiers and / or messages in one statement. For example:

```
Writeln (Number1, ' + ', Number2, ' = ', Sum);
```

Note the commas separating the different parts.

The Readln Statement

We frequently want programs to process values that are provided while the program is running. To store a value typed by the user in a variable we use the `Readln` statement with the variable identifier in brackets:

```
Readln (Number1)
```

To display the sum of two numbers that the user types in, we can write:

Figure 2.2: The program code

- Save your work by choosing **File, Save All** and making a new folder for this program.

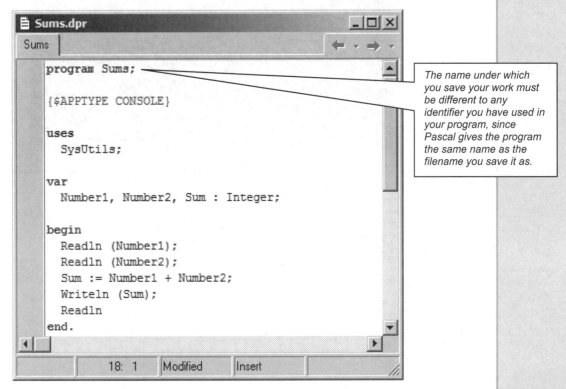

Figure 2.3: The saved program name

- Run this program.

This will produce the required result. However, it is not very user-friendly: we need to prompt the user for what to do.

- Add some lines to your program as follows:

```
begin
  Write ('Please type in a number: ');
  Readln (Number1);
  Write ('Please type in another number: ');
  Readln (Number2);
  Sum := Number1 + Number2;
  Writeln (Number1, ' + ', Number2, ' = ', Sum);
  Readln

end.
```
```
23: 4   Modified   Insert
```

Figure 2.4: Making the program more user-friendly

This will produce the following output:

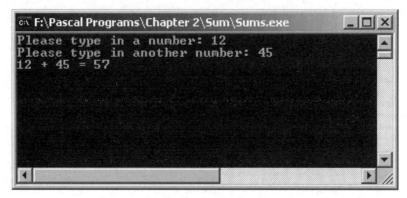

Figure 2.5: The Run window for the above program

Note: Writeln without parameters will just output a new line.
Write rather than Writeln will stay on the same line.

The statement

```
Writeln (Number1, ' + ', Number2, ' = ', Sum);
```

produces the same result as

```
Write (Number1);
Write (' + ');
Write (Number2);
Write (' = ');
Write (Sum);
Writeln;
```

Although the Read statement exists, its use is very specific as it leaves the **Enter** character in the input buffer. If you try it, your program may not operate as you expect.

Arithmetic Expressions

We can write more complicated arithmetic expressions, using the following symbols:

Arithmetic Operator	Operation	Operand data types	Result data type	Example
+	addition	integer, real	integer, real	X + Y
−	subtraction	integer, real	integer, real	Result - 1
*	multiplication	integer, real	integer, real	P * InterestRate
/	real division	integer, real	real	X / 2
DIV	integer division	integer	integer	Total DIV UnitSize
MOD	remainder	integer	integer	Y MOD 6

Note: Division using / will produce a result that may not be a whole number. We need to declare a variable receiving such a result as a *Real* data type, so that it may have a decimal point and a fractional part. For more data types, see the next chapter.

Comments

As a further aid to self-documentation, comments in the program code are a way to include notes about the purpose of the program or parts of the program. The compiler ignores these, so your application file (.*exe* file) is not taking up more memory as a result of comments.

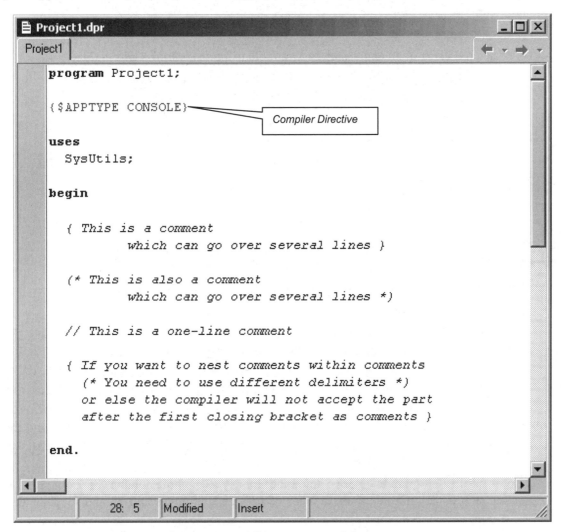

Figure 2.6: Different comment delimiters

Statements with a $ immediately after { or (* are not comments but compiler directives.

Printing out your program

If you want a hard copy of the program code you have written:

- Select **File, Print ...**

Summary

You have learnt to:

- ✓ declare variables using **var** *identifierlist* **:** *type*
- ✓ assign the value of an expression to a variable using *variable* : = *expression*
- ✓ assign a value typed in at the keyboard to a variable using `Readln` (*variable*)
- ✓ output the value of a variable using `Writeln` (*variable*) or `Write(`*variable*`)`
- ✓ comment your code using { } or (* *) or //
- ✓ distinguish comments from compiler directives such as {$APPTYPE CONSOLE}
- ✓ print your program code using **File, Print …**

Exercises

2.1 Write a program that will read in three integers and display the sum.

2.2 Write a program that will read two integers and display the product.

2.3 Enter the length, width and depth of a rectangular swimming pool. Calculate the volume of water required to fill the pool and display this volume.

2.4 `x DIV y` calculates how many times y divides into x, for example `7 DIV 3` is 2. `x MOD y` calculates the remainder that results after division, for example `7 MOD 3` is 1. Write a program that will read in two integers `Number1` and `Number2`. Using `DIV` and `MOD`, your program should display the whole number part and the remainder of dividing `Number1` by `Number2`. Make the display easy to understand for the user.

Hint: Use DIV and MOD

2.5 Write a program to enter an amount of money as a whole number, for example £78, and display the minimum number of £20, £10, £5 notes and £2 and £1 coins that make up this amount.

For example, the value £78 would give 3 twenty pound notes, 1 ten pound note, 1 five pound note, 1 two pound coin and 1 one pound coin.

Note: If Pascal does not display the £ sign when you use `Write('£')`, use `Write(Chr(156))` instead.

Chapter 3 – Data Types

All variables have to be declared before they can be used. The compiler will allocate memory to each variable depending on what type it is. Pascal provides many built-in types, some of which are listed below. In Chapter 9 you will learn how to define your own data types.

Integer

This data type supports positive and negative whole numbers. Memory allocated: 4 bytes. Range: -2147483648 to 2147483647. Whenever possible you should use *Integer* variables rather than *Real* variables, because they use less memory and they store values more accurately.

Byte

This data type supports unsigned integers in the range 0 to 255. Memory allocated: 1 byte.

Real

This data type supports signed numbers with a decimal point and fractional part, to a maximum of 15 to 16 significant digits. Memory allocated: 8 bytes.

Char

This is a single character. Memory allocated: 1 byte. You can assign a single character to a *Char* variable:

```
Letter1 := 'A'
```

String

A string is a sequence of characters. A string variable can store up to 2^{31} characters. However a string constant is limited to 255 characters.

`'Hello World'` `'012  34£$%^'`	Examples of string constants
`'Here''s how'`	if you want to include the apostrophe in a string literal you need to type two apostrophes
`' '`	this string literal contains a space
`''`	this string is known as a null string (it contains nothing)

You can assign a string literal to a string variable:

```
FirstName := 'Fred'
```

You can concatenate strings (join one string to the end of another) using the string operator +

```
Message := 'Hello ' + 'World'
FullName := FirstName + Surname
```

Currency

This data type minimizes rounding errors in monetary calculations. It is stored as an integer with the four least significant digits implicitly representing decimal places, as though you were calculating to the nearest hundredth of a penny. Memory allocated: 8 bytes.

Boolean

This data type supports just two values: **True** and **False**. For example:

```
Found := False
Finished := True
```

Memory allocated: 1 byte. Pascal represents **True** as 1 and **False** as 0 in memory. You will learn to use this data type in Chapters 4 and 5. The following Boolean operators can be used in expressions with Boolean variables:

Boolean operator	Logical operation	Explanation	Example assuming Found := True Finished := False	Value of example
not	inversion	turns **True** to **False** and vice versa	**not** Finished	True
and	AND	both values must be true for the result to be true	Found **and** Finished	False
or	inclusive OR	either or both values must be true for the result to be true	Found **or not** Finished	True
xor	exclusive OR	only one value must be true for the result to be true	Found **xor not** Finished	False

The results of a Boolean expression can be assigned to a Boolean variable. For example:

```
Searching := not Found or not Finished
GiveUp := not Found and Finished
```

TDateTime

This data type supports dates. Pascal stores the date as a real number. The integral part of a Pascal *TDateTime* value is the number of days that have passed since 12/30/1899. The fractional part of the *TDateTime* value is the fraction of a (24-hour) day that has elapsed.

You can perform calculations with date variables. If `Today` has today's *TDateTime* value stored:

```
Tomorrow := Today + 1
Yesterday := Today -1
```

To print out a date value you need to make a conversion (see Chapter 6).

Ordinal data types

Ordinal types include *integer, byte, character* and *Boolean*. An ordinal type defines an ordered set of values. These types are important in later chapters.

Simple data types

Simple types include ordinal types, *Real* and *Currency*. In Chapters 7 and 9, we will learn about types that are not simple types and are known as structured types. An example of a structured type is the *String* data type.

Displaying values from different variable types

As we saw on page 10, the `Write` and `Writeln` statements can write one or more values to the output window. These values can be string literals, strings or simple types.

Each value can also be followed by the specification of a minimum field width *m* and the number of decimal places *n*.

m must be greater than 0.

n specifies the number of decimal places for *Real* and *Currency* data types. For example:

```
Write (Cost:5:2)
```

will display the value held in `Cost` taking up 5 character spaces and to 2 decimal places.

Constants

If we want to use values that will not change throughout the program, we can declare them as constants rather than variables at the beginning of the program in the **const** section, where we also initialise them.

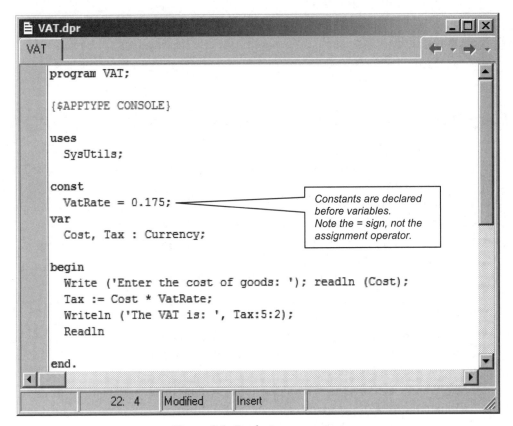

Figure 3.1: Declaring a constant

Advantages of using named constants rather than variables:

- o The value of a constant cannot be accidentally changed during the running of the program.
- o The program runs faster because all references to the constant are replaced by its value at compile time, whereas a variable's value has to be retrieved from main memory at run time.

Advantages of using a named constant rather than the actual value:

- o If the value needs to be changed at a later date, such as the VAT rate changes, only the constant declaration needs to be changed.
- o Expressions using the value are much easier to understand if a carefully chosen identifier represents the value.

Summary

You have met:

- ✓ Named constants
- ✓ Simple variable types
    - o Real, Currency, DateTime
    - o Ordinal types: Integer, Byte, Char, Boolean
- ✓ Structured variable types:
    - o String

Exercises

3.1 Write a program that will ask the user for their first name. The program should then concatenate the name with a message, such as 'Hello Fred. How are you?' and output this string to the user.

3.2 Write a program that asks the user to enter two real numbers and displays the product of these two numbers to 2 decimal places, with user-friendly messages.

3.3 Write a program to enter a temperature in degrees Fahrenheit and display the equivalent temperature in degrees Centigrade.
The formula for conversion is Centigrade = (Fahrenheit – 32) * (5/9).

3.4 Write a program to convert a person's height in inches into centimetres and their weight in stones into kilograms. [1 inch = 2.54 cm and 1 stone = 6.364 kg]

3.5 Write a program to enter the length, width and depths at the deepest and shallowest ends of a rectangular swimming pool. Calculate the volume of water required to fill the pool, and display this volume.

3.6 Write a program to enter the length and width of a rectangular-shaped garden. Calculate the area of the garden and the cost of turfing a lawn if a 1m border is around the perimeter of the garden. Assume the cost of turf is £10 per square metre. Display the result of these calculations.

Chapter 4 – Selection

We often want computers to take different routes through a program depending on various conditions. For this we can use one of the following **structured statements**[1] Pascal provides:

```
if ... then
if ... then ... else
case
```

If ... Then

When we want our program to execute a statement only if a certain condition is met, we use:

```
if BooleanExpression then statement
```

A **Boolean expression** returns a Boolean value **True** or **False** (see Chapter 3 for *Boolean type*). If the *BooleanExpression* is **True** the statement after **then** is executed.

Note:
*The mathematical expression
10 < X < 25
must be written as
(X > 10) **and** (X < 25)
in Pascal*

Examples of Boolean expressions:

```
Age > 18
Number > 10) and (Number <=25)
```

The brackets around the parts either side of logical operators are required

You can use the following comparison operators:

```
=     equal to
<>    not equal to
>     greater than
<     less than
>=    greater than or equal to
<=    less than or equal to
```

Example of an **if ... then** statement:

```
if Number > 0
   then Sum := Sum + Number
```

---

[1] You will meet other structured statements. Structured statements are built from other statements. We use a structured statement when we want to execute other statements sequentially, conditionally, or repeatedly.

Exercise

4.1 Write a program that asks for two numbers from the user and then displays a suitable message if the two numbers are the same.

If ... Then ... Else

When we want our program to do one statement if a certain condition is met, and another statement if the condition is not met, we use:

```
if BooleanExpression then statement1 else statement2
```

Example of an **if ... then ... else** statement:

```
if Number<0
   then Writeln('this is a negative number')
   else Writeln ('this is a positive or zero number')
```

Exercises

4.2 Write a program that will read in a person's age and display a message whether they are old enough to drive or not.

4.3 Write a program that checks whether a number input is within the range 21 to 29, inclusive, and displays an appropriate message.

4.4 Write a program that asks the user to enter 2 numbers and displays the larger of the two numbers.

Nested If statements

The statement in a **then** and/or **else** part of an **if** statement can itself be an **if** statement.

Example:

```
if ((Ch >= 'A') and (Ch <= 'Z')) or ((Ch >= 'a') and (Ch <= 'z'))
   then writeln ('letter')
   else
      if (Ch >= '0') and (Ch <= '9')
         then writeln ('numeral')
         else writeln ('special character');
```

Exercises

4.5 Extend program 4.3 so a number out of range will cause a message saying whether it is above or below the range.

4.6 Adapt program 4.4 to determine which is the largest of three given integers.

Compound statements

Sometimes we may want to have more than one statement in the **then** and/or **else** part of an **if** statement. We need to group these together into a compound statement.

A compound statement is a sequence of one or more statements to be executed in the order in which they are written. The reserved words **begin** and **end** serve as statement brackets. When bracketed in this way, any number of consecutive statements can be treated as a single statement.

```
begin
  statement1;
  statement2;
  ...
  statementn
end
```

What will be the output of the following piece of program code?

```
Number := 15;
if Number > 10
  then
    begin
      Writeln('You are a winner');
       Writeln('Please collect your prize');
    end
  else
    begin
      Writeln('Better luck next time');
    end;
```

Indentation

With the introduction of structured statements, we need to take care over the layout of our code, to keep it easy to find possible errors. Pascal does not mind where you put white space (spaces, indents, new lines). However, to follow the code, especially during error-finding sessions you will appreciate clearly laid out code. A good convention is:

➤ Every statement on a new line.

➤ Indent the statements within a compound statement and line up **begin** and **end**:

```
begin
    statement1;
    statement2;
    ...
    statementn
end
```

➤ A **begin** always must be matched by an **end**. However, some structured statements, such as the **case** statement, have an **end** without a matching **begin**. To make it easier to see that this **end** closes the case statement, add a comment (as in the example on the next page):

```
end {case}
```

➤ Split **if** statements and indent in this way:

```
if BooleanExpression
    then statement1
    else statement2
```

Note that there must be no semicolon here. This is a common syntax error.

➤ If you use compound statements in an if statement, indent in this way:

```
if BooleanExpression
    then
        begin
            statement1;
            ...
            statementn
        end
    else
        begin
            statementx
            ...
        end
```

Note that there must be no semicolon here. This is another common syntax error.

Case

Nested **if** statements can get very complicated and sometimes it is easier to use a **case** statement:

```
case OrdinalExpression of
  CaseList1: statement1;
    ...
  CaseListn: statementn;
else                          // else part
  statements;                 // optional
end {case}
```

The value of the *ordinal expression* (see Chapter 3, *Ordinal Type*) will determine which statement is executed. Each *CaseList* must be a constant, a list of constants or a subrange. Each value in the caselists must be unique in the case statement, and subranges[2] and lists must not overlap. See examples below.

If *Month* is an integer variable:

```
case Month of
  1, 3, 5, 7, 8, 10, 12 : NoOfDays := 31; // lists of
  4, 6, 9, 11           : NoOfDays := 30; // constants.
  2                     : NoOfDays := 28; // a constant.
end; {case}
```

If *Ch* is of type **Char**:

```
case Ch of
  'A'..'Z', 'a'..'z' : writeln ('letter');    // subranges
  '0'..'9'           : writeln ('numeral');   // subrange
  '+', '-', '*', '/' : writeln ('operator');  // constants
else
  writeln ('special character');              // optional
end; {case}
```

Exercises

4.7   Write a program that asks the user for a month number and displays the number of days that month has (ignore leap years for now).

4.8   Write a program that lets the user enter a number between 1 and 12 and displays the month name for that month number. The input *3* would therefore display March.

---

[2] You will learn more about subranges in Chapter 9

Summary

You have learnt to:

- ✓ Use **if … then … else** statements
- ✓ Write Boolean expressions
- ✓ Use the **case** statement in the format:

```
case OrdinalExpression of
  caseList1: statement1;

     ...

  caseListn: statementn;
else                        // else part
  statements;               // optional
end {case}
```

- ✓ Write compound statements using **begin** and **end** as statement brackets
- ✓ Indent code to make error finding easier

Exercises

4.9   Write a program that reads in the temperature of water in a container (in Centigrade) and displays a message stating whether the water is frozen, boiling or neither.

4.10 Write a program that asks the user for the number of hours worked this week and their hourly rate of pay. The program is to calculate the gross pay. If the number of hours worked is greater than 40, the extra hours are paid at 1.5 times the rate. The program should display an error message if the number of hours worked is not in the range 0 to 60.

4.11 Write a program that reads in an exam mark and displays the relevant grade. The grade boundaries are:

0 to 40 marks	grade U
41 to 50 marks	grade E
51 to 60 marks	grade D
61 to 70 marks	grade C
71 to 80 marks	grade B
81 to 100 marks	grade A

4.12 Extend your program for Exercise 4.7 to include leap years. A year is a leap year if the year divides exactly by 4, but a century is not a leap year unless it is divisible by 400. For example the year 1996 was a leap year, the year 1900 was not, the year 2000 was a leap year.

Hint: Use the operators DIV and MOD

4.13 Write a program that accepts a date as three separate integers such as 12 5 03. The program should display the date in the form 12th May 2003.

4.14 Adapt your program to interpret a date such as 12 5 95 as 12th May 1995. Your program should interpret the year to be in the range 1931 to 2030.

Chapter 5 – Iteration (Repetition)

We often want computers to repeat some process several times. This is called **iteration**. In Pascal there are 3 different structures to repeat a set of statements:

Definite Iteration (when we know before entering the loop how often we want to repeat)
   for loop

Indefinite Iteration (when we do not know beforehand how often we want to repeat)
   repeat loop
   while loop

For loop

```
for Counter := StartValue to EndValue
  do
    statement;
```

Counter is called the **control variable** and must be declared as an ordinal type, often integer (see Chapter 3).
StartValue & *EndValue* must be expressions of the same type as *Counter*.

Examples:
```
for Count := 1 to 10 do Writeln ('This is line ',Count)
for Counter := 10 downto 0 do Writeln (Counter);
for Letter := 'A' to 'Z' do Write (Letter);
```

If we want to repeat more than one statement, we need to use the compound statement:

```
for Counter := 1 to NoOfStudents do
begin
   Readln (Marks);
   RunningTotal:= RunningTotal + Marks;
end;
AverageMarks := RunningTotal / NoOfStudents;
```

Exercises

5.1 Make each of the four examples on the previous page into a program to test what it does.

5.2 Write a program that displays the word 'Hello' on the screen 4 times on the same line using the **for** loop.

5.3 Write a program that prompts the user to enter a short message and the number of times it is to be displayed and then displays the message the required number of times.

5.4 Write a program to display the squares of all the integers from 1 to 12 in two columns headed 'Number' and 'Square of Number'.

5.5 Write a program that asks the user to enter the number of stars per row and the number of rows to be displayed. For example, entering 5 and 3 should display:

      * * * * *

      * * * * *

      * * * * *

Hint: You can nest two loops inside each other, the inner loop to count the number of stars, and the outer loop to count the number of lines.

5.6 Write a program that asks for a number, and displays the squares of all the integers between 1 and this number inclusive.

5.7 Adapt your program from exercise 5.6 so that it will display 5 values on each line.

    Hint: Use `Write` to display a value and a statement of the form

        if `ControlVariable` **MOD** 5 = 0 **then** `Writeln;`

    to output a new line after every fifth value.

5.8 Write a program that asks the user to enter how many numbers are to be averaged, then enters this number of numbers, calculating the average. The program should display the average on the screen.

5.9 Write a program to display an 'n times table' for a given integer n. For $n = 4$, the output should be:

```
1 * 4 = 4
2 * 4 = 8
3 * 4 = 12
. . . .
12 * 4 = 48
```

5.10 **n factorial**, usually written **n!**, is defined to be the product of all the integers in the range 1 to n:

        n! = 1 * 2 * 3 * 4 * ....* n

    Write a program that calculates **n!** for a given positive n.

Repeat loop

```
repeat
  statement1;
  statement2;
  :
  :
until BooleanExpression
```

The statements enclosed by **repeat** and **until** are executed again and again until the *BooleanExpression* is **True**.

> **Note:** The statement sequence is executed at least once, even if *BooleanExpression* is already **True**.

Example:
```
repeat
  Write ('enter a name, XXX to finish');
  Readln (Name)
until Name = 'XXX';
```

We may wish to know how many times the loop was repeated:

```
Count := 0;
repeat Write ('enter a number, 0 to finish');
  Readln (Number);
  Count := Count + 1
until Number = 0;
```

If we want to add up all the numbers the user types in, we need to keep a running total:

```
Count := 0;            // always make sure you initialise
RunningTotal := 0;     // variables before using them
repeat write ('enter a number, 0 to finish');
  readln (Number);
  Count := Count + 1;
  RunningTotal := RunningTotal + Number
until Number = 0;
```

Exercises

5.11   Write a program that reads in a series of numbers and adds them up until the user enters zero. (This stopping value is often called a **rogue value**.)

5.12   Write a program that asks the user for a number between 10 and 20 inclusive and will validate, that is test, the input. It should repeatedly ask the user for this number until the input is within the valid range.

5.13   Expand your program from Exercise 5.11 to display the average as well as the sum of the numbers entered. Make sure you do not count the rogue value as an entry.

While loop

```
while BooleanExpression
  do statement;
```

While *BooleanExpression* is **True** the statement is repeatedly executed.

Note that the statement will not even be executed once, if *BooleanExpression* is already **False**.

Example

```
while Number < 0
  do Readln (Number);
```

Unlike the **repeat** loop, if we want to repeat more than one statement, we need to use a compound statement:

```
Writeln('Type in a positive number: ');
Readln(Number);
while Number <= 0
  do
    begin
      Writeln('This was not a positive number!')
      readln(Number)
    end;
```

Exercises

5.14   Write a program that asks a user for a number between 10 and 20 inclusive. The program should give the user a message if the number input is outside this range and ask for another number until the number input is within range.

5.15   Make changes to your program from Exercise 5.13, so it will also work if the user does not want to type in any numbers and uses the rogue value straight away.

Summary

You have learnt to use a:

✓ **for** loop when you know how many times you wish to repeat the loop:

```
for counter := StartValue to EndValue
   do
      statement;
```

✓ **repeat** loop when you don't know how many times you want the loop to be obeyed, but it must be **at least once:**

```
repeat
   statements;
   ...
until BooleanExpression
```

✓ **while** loop when you don't know how many times you want the loop to be obeyed, and it may not be at all:

```
while BooleanExpression
   do
      statement;
```

Exercises

5.16 Write a program that displays a conversion table for pounds to kilograms, ranging from 1 pound to 20 pounds [1 kg = 2.2 pounds].

5.17 Write a program that asks the user to enter 8 integers and displays the largest integer.

5.18 Adapt your program from Exercise 5.17 so that it will also display the smallest integer.

5.19 Write a program that takes two letters as input and displays all the letters of the alphabet between the two supplied letters (inclusive). For example, EJ produces EFGHIJ. The letters are to be printed in the order in which the specified letters are supplied. GB should produce GFEDCB.

5.20 Adapt your program from Exercise 5.17 so that the user can type in any number of positive integers. Input will terminate with the rogue value of –1.

5.21 Adapt your program from Exercise 5.20, if necessary, so that it works if the user types in the rogue value as the first value.

Chapter 6 – Functions

Built-in functions

A function is a routine, a self-contained statement block that returns a value when it executes. Pascal provides many ready-to-use functions. Here are just a few:

Function identifier	Parameter(s) (Arguments)	Result type	Description
Sqr	X: Integer	Integer	Returns the square of *X*
Sqr	X: Real	Real	Returns the square of *X*
Sqrt	X: Real	Real	Returns the square root of *X*
Round	X: Real	Integer	Returns the value of *X* rounded to the nearest whole number
Trunc	X: Real	Integer	Truncates a real number to an integer
Chr	X: byte	Char	Returns the character for a specified ASCII code value *X*
Ord	X: any ordinal type	Integer	Returns the ordinal value of an ordinal type expression such as the ASCII code for a character.
Length	S: String	Integer	Returns the number of characters in string *S*
Pos	Sub: String S: String	Integer	Returns the index value of the first character in substring *Sub* that occurs in string *S*
UpperCase	S: String	String	Returns a copy of string *S* in upper case
LowerCase	S: String	String	Converts string *S* to lower case
Date	-	TDateTime	Returns the current local date as a TDateTime value
DateToStr	TDateTime	String	Returns the string equivalent of *D*
StrToDate	S: String e.g. 12/2/03	TDateTime	If *S* contains only two numbers, it is interpreted as a date in the current year.
EoLn	-	Boolean	Returns **True** if the next character input is the end-of-line character, **False** otherwise.
From the **StrUtils** unit:			
ReverseString	S: String	String	Returns the reverse of string *S*
LeftStr	S: String L: Integer	String	Returns the substring of length *L* that appears at the start of string *S*
RightStr	S: String L: Integer	String	Returns the substring of length *L* that appears at the end of string *S*
MidStr	S: String P: Integer L: Integer	String	Returns the substring of length *L* that appears at position *P* in string *S*

For more routines look in **Delphi Help** under *ConvUtils, DateUtils, Math, StrUtils, System, SysUtils* routines and other units.

To use any of these functions you use its identifier and provide the necessary arguments in brackets. This is called the *function call*. A function call returns a value, which can be used in expressions in assignments and comparison operations. For example, to assign the square root of a number to *Square*:

Example:

```
Square := Sqr (Number)
```

You must make sure that you provide the correct data types.

Function calls cannot appear on the left side of an assignment statement.

Exercises

6.1   Write a program that asks the user to type in a number with decimal places. The program should then display the rounded and the truncated number.

6.2   Write a program that reads in a string and displays the number of characters in the string.

6.3   Write a program that displays the ASCII code for any given character.

6.4   Write a program that will display the character for a given ASCII code.

6.5   Write a program that asks the user for their surname and displays the surname in uppercase letters.

6.6   Write a program that displays today's date.

6.7   Write a program that reads in a date, converts it into date format, adds a day and displays the next day's date.

6.8   Write a program that asks the user for a word, and then displays the ASCII code for each letter in the word.

Hint: Process one character at a time, using **Read** rather than **Readln.** As the user types characters at the keyboard, the characters are stored in a buffer. When the user presses the **Enter** key, the buffer is made available to the *Read / Readln* procedure. *Read* will take individual characters from the buffer as required but leave the *end-of-line* character produced by the **Enter** key, in the buffer. You can use *EoLn* to check for the end-of-line character. To clear the input buffer use *Readln.*

6.9   Write a program that asks the user to enter a sentence, terminated by a full stop and the pressing of the **Enter** key. The program should count the number of words and display the result.

Hint: A word will end with a space or a full stop.

Delphi Units

If you want to use built-in functions from units other than the *System* and *SysUtils* units you need to specify these in the **uses** clause. For example, if we want to use the *ReverseString* function from the *StrUtils* unit :

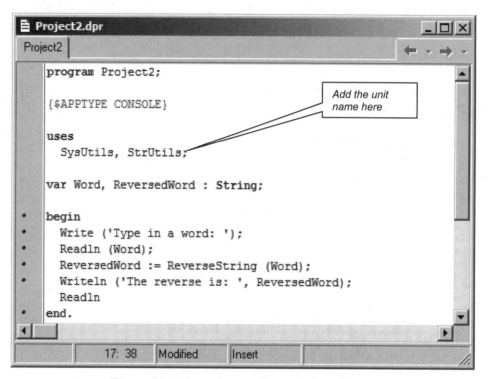

Figure 6.1: Using a function from the StrUtils unit

Exercises

6.10 Write a palindrome tester. A palindrome is a word or sentence that reads the same backwards as forwards. The user should enter a string and the program should display whether the string is a palindrome or not.

6.11 Write a program that asks the user for their first name and their surname. The program then displays the full name, first name capitalized (starting with a capital letter followed by lower-case letters) and surname, all uppercase, regardless of what case the user entered.

6.12 In the *DateUtils* unit, Delphi provides a function *YearSpan* to obtain the difference, in years, between two *TDateTime* values. The result is a real number. Write a program that reads in a date of birth and displays the user's age. Can you suppress the fractional part?

Random Numbers

We often want to simulate events where random numbers occur, such as throwing a die. Computers can only follow programs, that means sequences of predetermined statements, so they cannot produce truly random numbers. Pascal, like most high-level languages, provides us with a pseudo-random number generator to get over this problem. There are 2 random functions.

From the *System* unit which is always available:

```
Random (Last)
```

returns an integer between 0 (inclusive) and Last (exclusive).

From the *Math* unit (which you must specify in the **uses** clause):

```
RandomRange (First, Last)
```

returns an integer from the range that extends between First (inclusive) and Last (exclusive).

To initialise the random number generator using an integer obtained from the system clock so that you are highly likely to obtain the same sequence of numbers on any two runs, add the statement **Randomize** before you want to use one of the random functions:

```
var
  Number : integer;
begin
  Randomize;   // This should only be executed once to
               // initialise the random number generator
  Number := Random(6);   // generates a number 0 - 5
  Number := Number + 1;  // add 1 to get a number 1 - 6
  Writeln (Number);
  Readln
end.
```

For testing purposes you may wish to obtain the same sequence of numbers on each run. In this case, do not use Randomize; instead use RandSeed := *any integer value*.

Exercises

6.13 Write a program that will display random numbers between 1 and 6 until a six is generated.

6.14 Write a program that will display six random numbers between 5 and 10.

6.15 Write a game in which the user guesses what random number between 1 and 1000 the computer has 'thought of', until he or she has found the correct number. The computer should tell the user whether each guess was too high, too low or spot on.

User-defined functions

Delphi may not provide us with all the functions we may wish to use. We can declare our own functions and then call them in expressions just like built-in functions. They are known as user-defined, but in this case the user is the programmer using the programming language, not the end-user of the program.

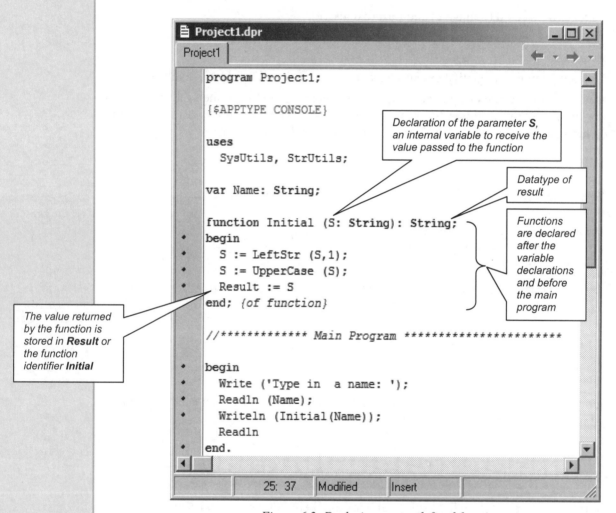

Figure 6.2: Declaring a user-defined function

Local Variables

Sometimes we need variables to store values temporarily. Rather than declaring variables that are available throughout the program (global variables), it is good programming style and less error-prone to declare variables locally. They can only be used in the function in which they are declared and we say that they have local scope.

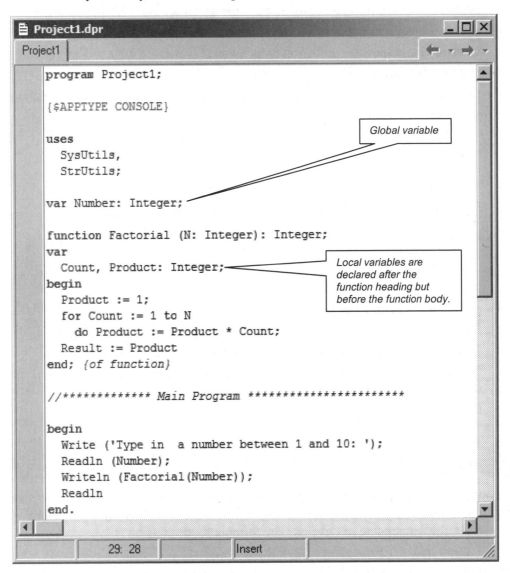

Figure 6.3: Declaring local variables in a function declaration

Summary

You have learnt:

- ✓ a function is a routine that is used in an expression because it returns a value
- ✓ how to use built-in functions
- ✓ the **uses** clause specifies units from which you may want to use a predefined routine
- ✓ to initialise the random number generator using *Randomize*
- ✓ to use the random number generator using the *Random* or *RandomRange* functions
- ✓ to declare your own functions using the format:

```
function Identifier (ParameterList): DataType;
var
   LocalDeclarations;
begin
   Statement1;      // function body must include a
   Statement2;      // statement that assigns a value
   .. ..            // to Result or the function's
   Statementn       // identifier
end {of function};
```

- ✓ to recognise global variables
- ✓ that global variables are available throughout the program
- ✓ to declare local variables between the routine heading and routine body
- ✓ that local variables are only available within the routine in which they are declared, which is known as their **scope**
- ✓ that using local variables reduces programming errors

Exercises

6.16 Write a function to convert temperatures from Fahrenheit to Celsius. The function should take one integer parameter (the temperature in Fahrenheit) and return a real result (the temperature in Celsius). The formula for conversion is

Centigrade = (Fahrenheit – 32) * (5 / 9)

6.17 Write a function that converts a string passed as a parameter into a capitalised string.

6.18 Write a function that returns the total number of seconds, calculated from a whole number of hours, minutes and seconds provided as 3 parameters.

6.19 Write your own random function *RandomNumber* that returns values in the range from 1 to the integer supplied as parameter.

6.20 Write a tables tester. The program chooses 2 random numbers and asks the user what is the product of these 2 numbers. If the user gets the answer wrong, the correct answer should be displayed. The program should ask 10 questions and then display a score out of 10 and a suitable message.

Chapter 7 – Arrays

High-level languages provide programmers with a variety of ways of organising data. There are not only simple data types, but also data structures.

A data structure is a data type composed of a number of elements of one or more data types. A data structure allows a variable to be declared of that type so that a number of data items can be stored and processed as a single set.

Various built-in and programmer-defined data structures allow the programmer to choose the data structure best suited to the type of processing to be carried out.

An array is an ordered set of data items of the same type grouped together using a single identifier. Arrays may have many dimensions but higher dimensions can get difficult to imagine and are not needed for AS or A-level. It is sufficient to be able to use one-dimensional arrays (also known as linear lists) and two-dimensional arrays (also known as tables).

The array's identifier and an index (or subscript) for each of the array's dimensions are used to refer to each of the array's data items.

Without data structures, if we want to store several values in separate variables and process them in a similar manner, this could result in very repetitive code. For example, to store 5 students' names would mean declaring 5 string variables for their names:

```
var Name1, Name2, Name3, Name4, Name5 : String;
```

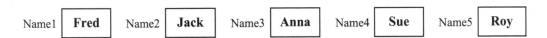

This is still manageable but what if we needed to store several hundred students' names?

One-Dimensional Arrays

If we declare an array:

```
var Name : array [1..5] of String;
```

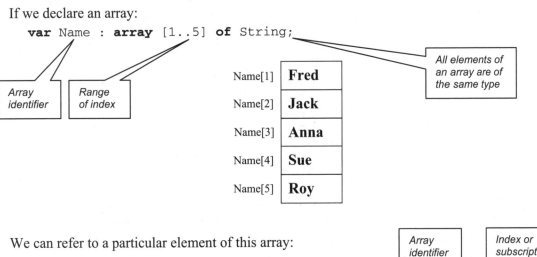

We can refer to a particular element of this array:

```
Writeln (Name[3])
```

would display the name Anna. In general, to refer to the ith element we write *Name[i]*

This is particularly powerful when combined with iteration statements:

To read in five names into the array we can write:

```
for Location := 1 to 5
  do
    begin
      Write ('Please type in name ', Location, ': ');
      Readln (Name[Location])
    end
```

We can easily display these names in reverse order:

```
for Location := 5 downto 1
  do Writeln (Name[Location])
```

In general, we declare a one-dimensional array using the format:

```
var identifier : array [range] of DataType
```

Range must be of ordinal type (see chapter 3). The following are examples of valid ranges for an array index:

```
1..12
-5..10
'A'..'Z'
```

Exercises

7.1   Write a program that reads 6 names into an array. The program must display the names in the same order that they were entered and then in reverse order.

7.2   We want to simulate throwing a die 30 times and record the scores. If we did this 'manually' we would end up with a tally chart:

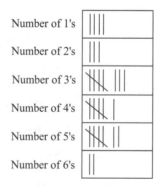

If we use a computer to keep a count of how many times each number was thrown, we could use an integer array (index range 1..6) instead of the tally chart. In general, a die throw will give a score i, and we want to increment the count in the ith element.

```
TallyChart[i] := TallyChart[i] + 1
```

Write a program to simulate the throwing of a die 30 times. The results of the simulation should be printed as a table of scores (1 to 6) and frequencies.

7.3   We wish to select six random numbers between 1 and 49 with the condition that all the numbers are different. One possible strategy, or algorithm, is:

*Initialise an array by using a **for** loop to store the values 1 to 49*

Repeatedly select a random element from array until a non-zero value is selected

Display this value

Set that element to zero

Repeat the above three steps until six numbers have been selected.

Write a program to select six unique random numbers between 1 and 49.

7.4   We can declare two arrays, *Student* and *DoB*, to store the name of Students and their dates of birth. For example if Fred is born on 22/12/84, then we could store 'Fred' in Student[1] and '22/12/84' in DoB[1]. To find a particular student we can use a repeat loop:

```
Ptr := 0;
repeat
  Ptr := Ptr + 1;
until (Student[Ptr] = WantedStudent) OR (Ptr = 5);
```

Write a program that stores 5 students' names and dates of birth and then searches for a particular student and displays that student's date of birth and current age. Display a suitable message if the student's details cannot be found.

Hint: use the built-in functions YearSpan and Date.

Two-Dimensional Arrays

Suppose we want to store a student's timetable:

	Mon	Tue	Wed	Thu	Fri
Lesson 1	Maths	Physics	Computing	Electronics	Maths
Lesson 2	Physics	Physics	Electronics	Maths	Physics
Lesson 3	Lunch	Lunch	Lunch	Lunch	Lunch
Lesson 4	Computing	Electronics	Maths	Computing	Computing

We can declare a two-dimensional array:

```
var Timetable : array [1..4, 1..5] of String;
```

The dimensions of an array are neutral. They do not represent anything until we decide what each dimension will represent, declaring an appropriate range in the corresponding index. To refer to the 4th lesson on a Tuesday, we could therefore write:

```
Timetable[4,2]
```

To display all lessons for a Wednesday (the 3rd day of the week):

```
Day := 3;
for Lesson := 1 to 4
  do Writeln (Timetable [Lesson, Day])
```

To display the whole timetable:

```
for Lesson := 1 to 4
        do
          for Day := 1 to 5
            do
              writeln(Timetable[Lesson, Day])
```

Summary

You have learnt to:

✓ declare 1-D arrays using:

var *Identifier* : **array** [*StartValue .. EndValue*] **of** *DataType*

✓ access a single 1-D array element using: *Identifier*[*Index*]

✓ access all array elements in turn using a **for** loop, for example:

for Pointer := 1 **to** 10 **do** Writeln(Name[Pointer])

✓ declare 2-D arrays using:

var *Identifier* : **array** [*RowRange, ColumnRange*] **of** *DataType*

using the convention that the first dimension represents rows and the second dimension represents columns.

✓ access a single 2-D array element using: *Identifier*[*RowIndex, ColumnIndex*]

✓ access all array elements in turn using 2 nested **for** loops

Exercises

7.5 Using the statements on the previous page, write a program which asks the user for the subjects done in each period for each day and then prints out the timetable with suitable headings.

7.6 Using a two-dimensional array, write a program that stores the names of ten countries in column 1 and their capitals in column 2. The program should then pick a random country and ask the user for the capital. Display an appropriate message to the user to show whether they are right or wrong.

7.7 Expand the program above to ask the user 5 questions and give a score of how many they got right out of 5.

7.8 Store in a 1-D array a set of 5 place names, and in a 2-D array the distances between the places. Ensure that the order of the places is the same in both arrays. When the names of 2 places are input, the distance between them is displayed. If they are not both in the table, a suitable message should be displayed.

7.9 A Latin Square of order *n* is an *n* x *n* array which contains the numbers 1, 2, 3, ..., n such that each row and column contain each number exactly once. For example the following diagram shows a Latin Square of order 4. You can see that each row can be obtained from the previous one by shifting the elements one place to the left.

1	2	3	4
2	3	4	1
3	4	1	2
4	1	2	3

Design and write a program to store such a Latin Square of a size given by the user. The program should also display the Latin Square.

Chapter 8 – Procedures

A routine is a self-contained statement block that can be called from different locations in a program. A function is a routine that returns a value in its name when it executes, and so a function call is used as part of an expression. A procedure is a routine that does not return a value in this way and a procedure call is treated like a statement. Delphi provides many built-in procedures, for example `Readln` and `Writeln`. However, we can also write our own procedures.

A procedure declaration has the form
```
procedure ProcedureName(ParameterList);
  LocalDeclarations;
  begin
    statements
  end; {of procedure}
```

During the development of a programmed solution to a problem we may write down an algorithm or stepwise strategy. Each step can be used as a procedure call, and the detailed processing of the solution is performed in the procedure. This makes the main program body easy to understand as the procedure calls reflect the algorithm.

Worked Example:

Write a program which would display a pyramid of '*':

```
          *
         * * *
        * * * * *
       * * * * * * *
      * * * * * * * * *
     * * * * * * * * * *
```

The solution to this problem can be broken down into the following steps:
```
Initialize number of spaces and stars
Repeat
  Output leading spaces
  Output line of stars
  Adjust number of spaces and stars
Until number of stars is the number required
```

```
program PyramidOfStars;
{$APPTYPE CONSOLE}
uses
  SysUtils, StrUtils;
var MaxNoOfStars, NoOfStars, NoOfSpaces : Integer;


procedure InitialiseNoOfSpacesAndStars;
begin
  Write ('How many stars should be at the base? ');
  Readln (MaxNoOfStars);
  NoOfSpaces := Max DIV 2;   //enough space to accommodate base
  NoOfStars := 1             // tip has just one star
end;


procedure OutputLeadingSpaces;
var Count: Integer;
begin
  for Count:= 1 to NoOfSpaces
    do Write (' ');                // no new line required
end;


procedure OutputLineOfStars;
var Count: Integer;
begin
  for Count:= 1 to NoOfStars
    do Write ('*');
  Writeln                    // move to next line
end;


procedure AdjustNoOfSpacesAndStars;
begin
  NoOfSpaces := NoOfSpaces - 1;
  NoOfStars := NoOfStars + 2
end;


//******* Main Program starts here **********
begin
  InitialiseNoOfSpacesAndStars;
  repeat
    OutputLeadingSpaces;
    OutputLineOfStars;
    AdjustNoOfSpacesAndStars;
  until NoOfStars > MaxNoOfStars;
  Readln
end.
```

Parameters

Those routines that do not rely on global variables are self-contained and easily reused in other programs. They also make it easier to find programming errors (logic errors) as each routine can be tested separately and will not interfere with other routines. Values required by routines are best passed to the routine by means of parameters. Routines can have any number of parameters, but the order must be the same in the routine declaration and the routine call.

The worked example from overleaf could be written:

```pascal
program PyramidOfStars; // to display a pyramid of stars
{$APPTYPE CONSOLE}
uses
   SysUtils, StrUtils;
var MaxNoOfStars, NoOfStars, NoOfSpaces : Integer;


procedure Initialise (var Spaces, Stars, Max : Integer);
begin
  Write ('How many stars should be at the base? ');
  Readln (Max);
  Spaces := Max DIV 2;   //enough space to accommodate base
  Stars := 1             // tip has just one star
end;


procedure OutputLeadingSpaces (Spaces : Integer);
var Count: Integer;
begin
  for Count:= 1 to Spaces
    do Write (' ');             // no new line required
end;


procedure OutputLineOfStars (Stars : Integer);
var Count: Integer;
begin
  for Count:= 1 to Stars
    do Write ('*');
  writeln                    // move to next line
end;


procedure Adjust (var Spaces, Stars : Integer);
begin
  Spaces := Spaces - 1;
  Stars := Stars + 2
end;
```

```
//******* Main Program starts here **********
begin
  Initialise (NoOfSpaces, NoOfStars, MaxNoOfStars);
  repeat
    OutputLeadingSpaces (NoOfSpaces);
    OutputLineOfStars (NoOfStars);
    Adjust (NoOfSpaces, NoOfStars);
  until NoOfStars > MaxNoOfStars;
  Readln
end.
```

With careful choice of identifiers the main program body is easy to understand. The routines are now self-contained and could even be put into a separate unit.

Look at the procedure headings again:

```
procedure Initialise (var Spaces, Stars, Max : Integer);
procedure OutputLeadingSpaces (Spaces : Integer);
procedure OutputLineOfStars (Stars : Integer);
procedure Adjust (var Spaces, Stars : Integer);
```

Procedures *Initialise* and *Adjust* differ from *OutputLeadingSpaces* and *OutputLineOfStars*. Parameters that pass a value back to the main program from the procedure must be declared as variable parameters with the keyword **var** in front of them, whereas those parameters that only pass a value into the procedure are known as value parameters.

Value and Variable Parameters

Value parameters are passed by value, while variable parameters are passed by reference.

If you pass a variable as a **value parameter**, the procedure or function copies the value of the calling program's variable to the procedure's parameter. Changes made to the copy have no effect on the original variable and are lost when program execution returns to the calling program.

If a parameter is passed as a **variable parameter**, a pointer referring to the address in main memory of the original variable is passed. Changes made to the parameter within the body of the routine are made to the original variable, so in effect the new value is passed back to the program where the routine was called.

Summary

You have learnt to use procedures to:

- ✓ give a set of statements a name, this makes the code easier to understand (transparent)
- ✓ avoid repeating code, as the procedure can be called from anywhere in the program
- ✓ use parameters to pass data within programs
- ✓ use value parameters when a return value is not required
- ✓ use variable parameters when a value is to be passed back to the main program

Exercises

8.1 Write and test a procedure *Swap*, which takes two integers as parameters and returns the first value passed to the procedure as the second value returned by the procedure and vice versa.

8.2 Write and test a procedure *OutputSymbols*, which takes two parameters: an integer n and a character *symbol*. The procedure is to display, on the same line, the symbol n times. For example, the call `OutputSymbols(5,'#')` should display #####.

8.3 Write and test a procedure *Sort*, which takes two integers as parameters and returns them in ascending order.

For example, if *No1* contained 5 and *No2* contained 3, then the call *Sort(No1, No2)* will leave the value 3 in *No1* and the value 5 in *No2*, but the call *Sort(No2, No1)* will leave the variable contents as they are.

8.4 Using procedures, write a program that asks the user to enter an odd number, validates the number and then print an inverted pyramid of stars based on that number. For example, entering the value 5 will produce:

```
* * * * *
  * * *
    *
```

8.5 Using procedures, write a program that asks the user to enter an odd number, validates the number, and then displays a diamond of stars based on that number. For example, the value 7 would produce:

```
      *
    * * *
  * * * * *
* * * * * * *
  * * * * *
    * * *
      *
```

8.6 The game 'Last one loses' is played by two players and uses a pile of n counters. Players take turns at removing 1, 2 or 3 counters from the pile. The game continues until there are no counters left and the winner is the one who does **not** take the last counter. Using procedures, write a program to allow the user to specify n in the range 10 – 50 inclusive and act as one player, playing at random until fewer than 5 counters remain. Try playing against your program, and then playing to win.

8.7 Write a program to let the computer guess a number the user has thought of, within a range specified by you as the programmer.

8.8 Convert the program you wrote for Exercise 7.3 into a procedure *GetLotteryNumbers* that will supply 6 unique random numbers between 1 and 49.

Chapter 9 – Records
and User-Defined Types

Records

A record data type is a structured type. A record is a collection of variables, which need not all be of the same type and with no associated ordering. The variables can be regarded as fields of the record. Before we can use records we need to define what type of record we want, that is, what fields our record is going to have and what type of data we are going to store in them.

The syntax of a **record type** declaration is:

```
type Identifier = record
  fieldlist1: type1;
  fieldlist2: type2;
  .. ..
  fieldlistn: typen
end; {of record type declaration}
```

Type declarations must be placed before global **var** declarations. Once the type is declared we can declare variables of this new type just as we declared variables using types from chapter 3. A useful naming convention is to prefix a type with T, so a record type to store student details would be called *TStudent*::

```
type TStudent = record
  FirstName: String[15];
  Surname: String[25];
  DepositPaid: Currency;
  DateOfBirth: TDateTime
end; {of TStudent}
```

> Adding [n] after the string type, declares the string variable as a variable holding a fixed-length string of n characters.
> This makes the record into a fixed-length record. Important when saving to files (see Chapter 10).

Declare record variables of type *Tstudent*:
```
var Student1, Student2: TStudent;
```

Now we can access individual fields of this record variable:

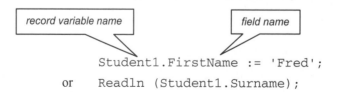

```
        Student1.FirstName := 'Fred';
or      Readln (Student1.Surname);
```

If accessing several fields of a record in succession, it can get tedious to write the full record name each time. Instead we can use the **with** statement.

With statement

A **with** statement can be used as a shorthand method for accessing the fields of a record.

```
With Student1
   do Readln (FirstName, Surname);
```
is equivalent to
```
Readln (Student1.FirstName, Student1.Surname);
```

```
with Student2
   do
     begin
       FirstName := 'Joe';
       Surname := 'Bloggs'
       DateOfBirth := StrToDate('1/4/1979')
     end {of with}
```
is equivalent to
```
Student2.FirstName := 'Joe';
Student2.Surname := 'Bloggs';
Student2.DateOfBirth := StrToDate('1/4/1979')
```

We can copy the values of one record's fields into another record of the same type.
```
Student2 := Student1
```
There is no need to transfer each field individually.

Exercises

9.1 Declare a record type to store the name of a country, the name of its currency and the exchange rate to the £. Write a program that reads in the details of one country and displays them formatted in a user-friendly way.

9.2 Extend your program from Exercise 9.1 to read in 3 countries and their respective details and display them in tabulated format.

9.3 Declare a record type to store the following employee details:

Employee name, employee number, total hours worked this week, hourly rate of pay.

Write a program that allows the user to enter an employee's data and displays a simple pay slip with the above details and the calculated weekly gross pay.

Arrays of Records

Just as with standard variables, when we want to work with a large collection it is better to access them by a collective name. Rather than declaring separate variables *Student1*, *Student2*, *student3*, … we can declare an array of student records, using the record type previously defined

```
var Student : array [1..500] of TStudent.
```

To assign a value to the first name of the 5th student in the array:

```
Student[5].FirstName := 'Jack'
```

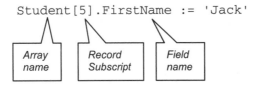

| Array name | Record Subscript | Field name |

Now we can use a **for** loop to access all the students' details:

```
for Ptr := 1 to NoOfStudents
  do
    Writeln(Student[Ptr].FirstName, Student[Ptr].Surname)
```

Exercises

9.4 Extend your program from Exercise 9.1 to store details of 10 countries in an array of records. Display the details in tabulated format.

9.5 Extend your program from Exercise 9.3 to store details of 15 employees. The program should be able to search by employee number and display that particular employee's pay slip. Display a suitable message if the employee cannot be found.

9.6 Declare an array *Student* of record type *TStudent* as above. Write a program to store 5 students' details. Enter 5 students' details and display their details in tabulated format.

9.7 Write a program that reads in an unspecified number, not exceeding 100, of friends' first names and ages into records. The program should then calculate the average age of your friends and display the average age correct to 2 decimal places. It should then display each of your friends' names and whether they are older or younger than the average age.

User-defined Types

When you declare routines that take array parameters, you cannot include index type specifiers in the parameter declarations. That is, the declarations

```
procedure Sort(Names: array of String);   //ERROR
```

or `procedure Sort(Names: array [1..100] of String);`

cause an error. However, if you declare the array as a type first, then you can use the type for the parameter declaration.

```
type TNames = array[1..100] of String;
procedure Sort(Names: TNames);
```

Exercises

9.8   We can declare the following array as a type, so that we can pass it as a parameter between routines:

```
type TLotteryNumbers = array[1..6] of Integer;
// declare variables as arrays of type TLotteryNumbers
var Draw1, MyLotteryNumbers: TLotteryNumbers;
```

Then we can use these variables as parameters in procedure calls:

```
GetLotteryNumbers(Draw1);
Check(MyLotteryNumbers, Draw1);
```

Adapt the procedure *GetLotteryNumbers* from Exercise 8.8 and write a program to store the numbers from a series of 10 weekly draws in an array of records. Each record should consist of an array of 6 integers (the drawn numbers) and the date of the draw. The program should ask the user for their 6 lucky numbers and then check through the 10 draws stored to see whether the user has won the jackpot. Display a suitable message.

User-defined types can aid program transparency. We distinguish between *enumerated types* and *subrange types*.

Enumerated Types (Ordinal / Symbolic)

Enumerated types define ordered sets of values by enumerating (or specifying) the values. Because enumerated types are ordinal types they may be used for **for** loop control variables, **case** statement selectors and array subscripts.

Examples

```
type
   TSuit = (Club, Diamond, Heart, Spade);
   TSeason = (Spring, Summer, Autumn, Winter);
   TDay = (Sun, Mon, Tue, Wed, Thu, Fri, Sat);
   TDirection = (North, East, South, West);
```

These types can then be used to declare variables:

```
var
   NewDirection, CurrentDirection  : TDirection;
   Day: TDay;
```

We can use members of these types as subscripts for arrays:

```
var HoursWorked = array [Mon..Fri] of Integer;
```

We can use members of these types as **for** loop control values:

```
for Day := Mon to Sun
  do
    Readln (HoursWorked[Day]);
```

We can use members of these types as **case** values:

```
case Day of
  Mon..Fri: Pay := HoursWorked[Day]* PayRate;
  Sat:      Pay := HoursWorked[Day]* PayRate * 1.5;
  Sun:   Pay := HoursWorked[Day]* PayRate * 2;
end {of case}
```

Symbolics can neither be written nor read directly. To translate input, ask for a code and convert this:

```
Write ('type N for North, E for East, ')
Write ('S for South, W for West: ');
Readln (DirectionCode);
case DirectionCode of
   'N' : NewDirection := North;
   'S' : NewDirection := South;
   'E' : NewDirection := East;
   'W' : NewDirection := West;
else
   Writeln ('incorrect input')
end; {case}
```

In a similar manner the symbolics can be output:

```
case CurrentDirection of
   North: Writeln ('North');
   South: Writeln ('South');
   East: Writeln ('East');
   West: Writeln ('West');
end; {case}
```

Exercises

9.9   Declare a symbolic type *TMonth*.

9.10 Declare the type *TDay* and the array *HoursWorked* from the previous page. Using these, write a program to collect the hours worked by an employee in a week and the hourly pay rate. The program should calculate and display the total hours worked and the gross pay for the week, assuming time-and-a-half on Saturdays and double-time on Sundays.

Subrange Types

We can declare types, which are subranges of any ordinal type. Therefore, subrange types are also ordinal types and can be used in **case** statements, as **for** loop control variables and array subscripts.

Examples:

```
type
  TCapitalLetter = ('A' .. 'Z'); // subrange of type Char
  TDigit = ('0' .. '9');          // subrange of type Char
  TWeekday = (Mon .. Fri);        // using enumerated type TDay
```

These types can then be used to declare variables:

```
var Weekday: TWeekday;
```

We can use members of these types as **for** loop control values:

```
for WeekDay := Mon to Fri
  do
    Readln (HoursWorked[WeekDay])
```

Exercises

9.11   Using your month type from Exercise 9.9, define the subrange types *TWinterMonth*, *TSpringMonth*, *TSummerMonth*, *TAutumnMonth*.

9.12   Declare a subrange type *TLetters* and an array *LetterFrequency,* write a program that counts the number of occurrences of each letter in a paragraph of text.

Hint: Don't distinguish between upper case and lower case letters for the purposes of counting the number of occurrences of the letters. Convert all letters to lower case first.

Summary

You have learnt to:

- ✓ declare record types using the format

  ```
  type Identifier = record
      fieldlist1: type1;
      fieldlist2: type2;
      .. ..
      fieldlistn: typen
  end; {of record type declaration}
  ```

- ✓ declare record variables using a previously declared record type
- ✓ access a single field using the format *RecordVariableName.FieldName*
- ✓ use the **with** statement as shorthand to access fields of a record
- ✓ declare arrays of records using a previously defined record type
- ✓ declare an array as a type so it can be passed as a parameter to a routine
- ✓ declare enumerated data types
- ✓ declare subrange data types
- ✓ use enumerated type and subrange type values in **case** statements and as **for** loop control variables

Chapter 10 – Files

So far, we have lost any data the user typed in during the running of the program. If we want to keep data from one time of running a program to the next, we need to save it in a computer file. A file is a sequence of elements of the same type. Delphi supports text files, typed files and untyped files. We will not consider untyped files further in this book.

Steps to use a file:

- ➤ Declare a file variable (see *text files* below or *typed files* on page 61)
- ➤ Assign external file name: `AssignFile (FileName,'extFileName');`
- ➤ Open existing file: `Reset (FileName);`
  - **Or** create and open a new file: `Rewrite (FileName);`
- ➤ Read from the file: `Read (FileName, VariableList);`
  - **Or** write to the file: `Write (FileName, VariableList);`
- ➤ Close the file: `CloseFile (FileName);`

Text Files

A text file represents a file containing a sequence of characters formatted into lines, where each line is terminated by an end-of-line marker. A text file can be opened and read in a text editor.

To declare a variable of the built-in *TextFile* type:

```
var FileName : TextFile;
```

With text files, we also have the use of `Readln`, which will read data elements including the end-of-line marker, and `Writeln`, which saves an end-of-line marker after any data elements saved.

To create and write to a text file 'Test.txt'	To read from the text file 'Test.txt'

`var FileA : TextFile;`
`...`
`AssignFile (FileA, 'Test.txt');`
`Rewrite (FileA);`
`Writeln (FileA, 'Hello!');`
`CloseFile (FileA);`
	`var FileA : TextFile;`
	`...`
	`AssignFile (FileA, 'Test.txt');`
	`Reset (FileA);`
	`//check for end of file:`
	`while not EoF(FileA)`
	`  do`
	`    begin`
	`      Readln (FileA, Message);`
	`      //display on screen:`
	`      Writeln (Message);`
	`    end;`
	`CloseFile (FileA);`

Exercises

10.1 Write a program that reads in 5 lines of text the user types in at the keyboard. As each line is typed in, the program should write the line to a text file, using *Readln* and *Writeln*.

10.2 Write a program that reads lines of text from a text file and displays them to the user. You can create a text file in any text editor. Save it in the same folder as the code for this program. Remember to use *Eof (FileName)* to check when you reach the end of the file.

Sending a Text File to the Printer

Instead of assigning the internal file name to an external file name, we use the procedure call:

```
AssignPrn (TextFileVariable);
```

This causes all information written to *TextFileVariable* to be directed to the printer. After the variable is assigned, the program must call the `Rewrite` procedure to create and open the file.

The *AssignPrn* procedure is in the *Printers* unit, so remember to specify this in the **uses** clause.

If you also specify the *Graphics* unit in the **uses** clause, you can set the font, font style and font size. You can list as many style constants as required; to clear the styles use the empty list []. Font styles available are *fsBold, fsItalic, fsUnderline* and *fsStrikeOut*.

`Printer.NewPage` will start a new page.

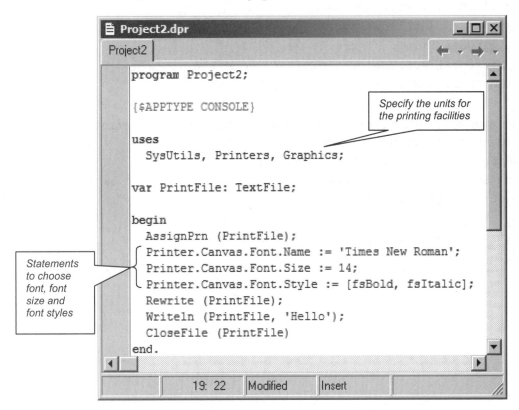

Figure 10.1: Sending output to the default printer

Exercise

10.3 Write a program that reads a message from the keyboard and then sends this message several times to the printer in different fonts, font sizes and styles.

Typed Files

We can declare a file of a previously declared record type.

For example, declare a record type *TStudent*:

```
type
  TStudent = record
    FirstName: String[15]; // Typed files can only handle
    Surname: String[25];   // fixed-length records
    DepositPaid: Currency;
    DateOfBirth: TDateTime
  end; {of record}
```

And now we can declare a file of this record type, and a record variable:

```
var
  StudentFile : file of TStudent;
  StudentDetails : TStudent;
```

To save a record to the new file declared above:

```
AssignFile (StudentFile, 'Student.dat');
Rewrite (StudentFile); // create new file
Write (StudentFile, StudentDetails); // save the record
CloseFile (StudentFile);
```

We can write as many records to the file as we like before closing the file. For example, we can save all the records in an array of records *StudentList* to a file:

```
AssignFile (StudentFile, 'Student.dat');
Rewrite (StudentFile); // create new file
for Count := 1 to NoOfRecords
  do
    Write (StudentFile, StudentList[Count]);
CloseFile (StudentFile);
```

To read records from a file into an array of records:

```
AssignFile (StudentFile,'Student.dat');
Reset (StudentFile); // open file for reading
Ptr := 0;
while not Eof (StudentFile)
  do
    begin
      Ptr := Ptr +1;
      Read (StudentFile,StudentList[Ptr]);
    end;
CloseFile (StudentFile);
```

Exercises

Serial Files

10.4 Declare a record type to store names and dates of birth. Write a program that reads a name and date of birth typed in at the keyboard and saves it to an external file.

10.5 Extend your program from the exercise above to read in several names and dates of birth and save each record out to the external file as it is entered. Allow the user to terminate input by pressing the **Enter** key without typing in a name.

10.6 Write a program that reads the file created in Exercise 10.4 and displays the record.

10.7 Write a program that reads the file created in Exercise 10.5 and displays the records as a table of names and dates of birth.

10.8 Write a program that reads records from the file created in Exercise 10.5 until it finds a specified name. The program should then display the name and corresponding date of birth. The program should display a suitable message if the name cannot be found in the file.

10.9 Write a program that will delete a specified record from the file created in Exercise 10.5.

Note: You cannot just delete a record in a serial or sequential file. You need to copy all records to a new file, omitting the specified record.

Sequential Files

10.10 Create a file with records in alphabetical order of name. Now write a program that will add a record in the correct position in the file.

Note: You cannot insert a record in a serial or sequential file. You need to copy records from the original file to a new file, inserting the new record in the correct place.

10.11 Write a program that reads the file created in Exercise 10.10 and searches for a specified name. If the name does not exist in the file, the program should abort the search at the earliest possible time and display a suitable message.

10.12 Write a program that will display a set of options to the user to add, delete or search for a record. Use the programs developed above to produce a fully working system.

Direct Access Files

The disadvantages with serial and sequential files are that you must start a search for a record from the beginning of the file, and adding or deleting records means writing all the records to a new file.

Direct access files (also known as random access files) do not store records one after the other but each record is stored at an address (or position relative to the start of the file) calculated from the value of its key field. This means a record can be independently accessed using its address. Since Pascal only allows fixed-length records, we can **update in situ** (overwrite an existing record with an updated record) without disrupting the file.

For example, if we wish to store details about stock items and these each have a unique item code (or primary key) between 0 and 1000, and then this item code could be used directly as the unique record address.

```
program DirectAccessFileExample;

{$APPTYPE CONSOLE}

uses
  SysUtils;

type
  TStockItem = record
                 StockItemCode : Integer;
                 Description : String[25];
                 UnitPrice : Currency;
                 NoInStock : Byte;
               end; {record}

var
  StockItem : TStockItem;
  StockFile : file of TStockItem;
  Position : Integer;

begin
  AssignFile (StockFile, 'Stock.dat');
  Reset (StockFile); // opens existing file
  Write ('Enter description: (X to finish) ');
  Readln (StockItem.Description);
```

```
     while StockItem.Description <> 'X'
       do
         begin
           Write ('Enter stock item code (0 to 1000): ');
           repeat
             Readln (StockItem.StockItemCode);
           until (StockItem.StockItemCode >=0)
                 and (StockItem.StockItemCode <= 1000);
           Write ('Enter unit price: ');
           Readln (StockItem.UnitPrice);
           Write ('Enter number of items in stock: ');
           Readln (StockItem.NoInStock);
           Position := StockItem.StockItemCode;
           // go to record position in file
           Seek (StockFile, Position);
           // write record to file at this address
           Write (StockFile,StockItem);
           Write ('Enter description: (X to finish) ');
           Readln (StockItem.Description);
         end;
     CloseFile (StockFile);
   end.
```

Often, the primary key for a set of records may be in a range not directly suitable as record addresses. For example, if the stock item codes were in the range 1000 to 9999, the first 999 record spaces in the file would never be used, so wasting a lot of disk space. In such a case, the primary key could be used in a calculation to produce a more suitable address. Such a calculation is called a **hashing algorithm** or **hashing function**. The primary key may not be numerical, again making it necessary to produce an address through some calculation on the primary key. It is important to design a hashing algorithm in such a way that it will produce the required range of record addresses, gives a good spread of addresses and minimises the number of different record keys that will produce the same record address (known as a **collision** or **synonym**). If we know that there will at most be 900 different stock items and the stock item codes are in the range 1000 to 9999, we might wish to generate addresses in the range 0 to 999. This could be done by taking the remainder after dividing the stock item code by 1000. Below is the function that could be called to give *Position* a valid address:

```
function Hash (Code: Integer):Integer;
   begin
     Result := Code MOD 1000;
   end;
```

We can also read an existing record by calculating its address using the same hashing function.

If a hashing function might produce synonyms, the program needs to check that the record space is vacant before writing a record at a given address. Similarly, when reading a record from a given address, the program needs to check that it is the required record. Provision can be made for synonyms by storing subsequent records that hash to the same address in the next free record space, wrapping to the beginning of the file when the end of the file has been reached.

Exercises

10.13 Type the program *DirectAccessFileExample* as a console application and test it.

10.14 Write a program to read the file created by the program from Exercise 10.13. The program should find a record when its primary key is supplied.

10.15 Modify your programs from Exercises 10.13 and 10.14 to use the hashing function on page 64.

10.16 Extend your programs so that they will be able to handle record keys that produce synonyms.

Summary

You have learnt to:

✓ declare text file variables

    var *FileName* : TextFile;

✓ declare typed file variables

    var *FileName* : **file of** *RecordType*;

✓ assign an external file name to a file

    AssignFile(FileName, 'ExternalFileName');

✓ open an existing file using   Reset (*FileName*);

✓ create and open a new file using   Rewrite (*FileName*);

✓ read from a file using   Read (*FileName*, *VariableList*);

✓ write to a file using   Write (*FileName*, *VariableList*);

✓ close a file using   CloseFile (*FileName*);

✓ send text to the printer by assigning the default printer to a text file using AssignPrn (*TextFileName*);

✓ go to a record directly using   Seek (*FileName*, *RecordAddress*);

✓ use a hashing function to calculate a record address from its primary key value

Chapter 11 – Consolidation Exercise

Write a program to implement a **simplified** payroll system for a small company.

The program should be able to work with data for up to 15 employees. Employees are paid weekly and receive an itemised payslip listing the hours they work, overtime done, gross pay, tax and national insurance and net pay after deductions.

Your program should also store the employee name and National Insurance Number. There is no need to store data for more than one week. It should be possible to search for an individual employee's details stored and preview their payslip details.

Your program should ensure that only valid data can be entered.

Assume the following fixed data:

- standard pay rate: £ 9.00 per hour
- overtime rate: £13.50 per hour
- normal working week: 37 hours
- maximum working week: 48 hours
- National Insurance: 11% of gross pay between £89 and £595 per week
- Tax is calculated using the following method:

    multiply gross pay by 52 to calculate annual pay

    apply tax rates to annual pay using the tax bands given below

    divide the resulting tax by 52 to calculate the week's income tax.

Tax bands as for tax year 2003 - 2004	
first £4,615	tax free
next £1,920	10%
£1,921 to £29,900	22%
over £29,900	40%

Part 2

Learning to Program in Delphi

In this section:

Chapter 12 – Introduction to Delphi

Traditional programming (such as when using Pascal) is essentially linear and based on the flow of execution. Programmers are responsible for all aspects of their program, including the screen display and user interface, and must write the code to do everything. If they want particularly elegant screen effects, then they have their work cut out. Programs are usually designed from top down, perhaps following the Jackson Structured Programming method, by breaking down complex operations into successively simpler ones.

Delphi is **object-oriented**, that means it revolves around ready-made objects. It is **event-driven** – that means all the activities in a program are triggered by one event or another. Each object has its own properties, determining its position, size, colour, the appearance and nature of its text and much more. Each object also has its own **event-handling procedures**. The Delphi system knows all about these already. It knows what a button is and how it works. It also knows how to handle text boxes, images, menus, option buttons and dialog boxes, and what happens when events occur. That event might be the opening of a form, the user clicking on a button or typing text into a box. The programmer does not have to write code to *trap* these events, the system does that automatically. Because the program code runs in response to events, and as at any point a whole range of events might be possible, the flow of execution is not fixed as in traditional programs.

Operations do not have to follow a set sequence. The process of program design reflects the nature of the system. You begin by creating the screen layout (the user-interface) and work outwardly from here, adding first the code that will run in response to specific events and then necessary code to co-ordinate the whole program.

A Delphi project

For any one application Delphi creates a number of files. For ease of working it is essential to create a directory for each application and then store all the files associated with it in this directory. Some of the files Delphi creates are:

File	Default Name	Extension
Project*	Project1	.dpr
- project configuration file	Project1	.cfg
- Delphi Options file	Project1	.dof
- resources file*	Project1	.res
Object Pascal code*	Unit1	.pas
Form*	Unit1	.dfm
Compiled Code	Unit1	.dcu
Executable file	Project1	.exe

---

* Do not delete these files, as your application may no longer work if you do.

The Delphi Environment

- Launch Delphi 7.
- You will now see a group of windows that make up the Delphi IDE (Integrated Development Environment). It is useful to take just a little time to familiarise yourself with these windows.

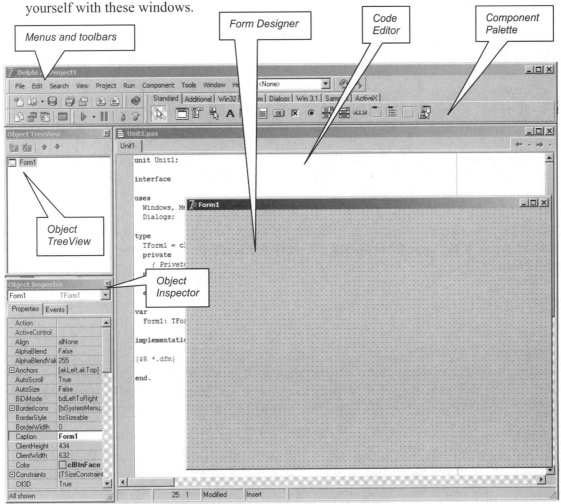

Figure 12.1: The Delphi Integrated Development Environment

Form Designer Window

The Form Designer Window is where you place components (**Edit** boxes, **Labels**, **Buttons**, **RadioButtons**, **CheckBoxes**, etc.) that make up the **interface** of your application. These components control the way in which the program runs and so what the program does. The interface is what you see in each window that opens when the application (program) is running.

The components are first selected from the Components Palette and then placed on the form. The location and size of the component can be set by changing the component's properties (**Left/Top** and **Width/Height**) or by dragging it with the mouse.

When you begin a new project, Delphi gives you a new form with the default name *Form1*. You can have as many forms in a project as your application needs and you save them as separate files. Remember to use meaningful names for these forms, as one of the advantages of a programming environment like Delphi is that any previously created form can be incorporated directly into any future project and will work immediately.

Component Palette

The components are grouped into categories under various page tabs.

The Standard Page Components

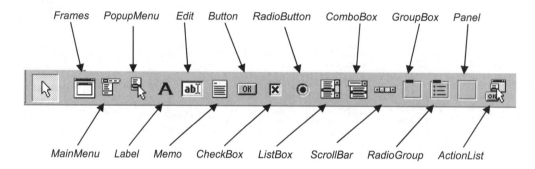

Figure 12.2: Standard Page Components

Each component has specific **properties**, **events** and **methods** that enable you to control your application.

Some examples of properties are as follows:

Property	Description
Name	All components have a Name property. This identifies them in any program code that you write. The default name for a component is usually something like *Form1, Command1, Text1,* etc. You will be renaming components later.
Caption	The Caption is the text that appears on or next to a component.
Font	The Font type as well as size, bold, italic, etc. can be set as in any application
Color	You will have to get used to American spellings. The component's colour can be changed to a range of different colours to enhance the appearance of the application.
Visible	This determines whether the component is in view on the screen at any particular time. For example, a label with a message can be made to appear or disappear depending on whether the message needs to be displayed or not.

You can scroll through the properties of any component to get an idea of what is available. You will learn how to set and use many of them in this book.

Object Naming Conventions

As mentioned earlier, when creating components in Delphi a default **Name** property is set for the component. However, it is much more desirable to give a more complete and meaningful name to each component. We are going to use the **Hungarian Notation**: this uses a prefix with each identifier that represents the identifier type. (See Appendix D.)

So for example if a form's main function is to act as a Save Window it would be useful to name the form *frmSave*, where *frm* is a prefix indicating that the object is a form and **Save** indicates what the form does.

Another example would be to name a **Close** button as *btnClose*.

The table below shows a recommended naming convention for some components:

Component	Prefix	Example
TButton	btn	btnExit
TCheckBox	chk	chkCommission
TComboBox	cbo	cboCustomers
TEdit	edt	edtEnglish
TForm	frm	frmCurrency
TGroupBox	grp	grpStyles
TLabel	lbl	lblEnglish
TListBox	lbo	lboCustomers
RadioGroup	rgrp	rgrpColour
TImage	img	imgLogo
TMaskEdit	medt	medtPostCode
TShape	shp	shpBox
TTimer	tmr	tmrResponse
TMemo	mem	memDetails
TLabeledEdit	ledt	ledtName

Creating an Application in Delphi

There are 3 main steps to creating an application in Delphi:

- **Create the interface**
- **Set the properties**
- **Write the code**

Getting Started

To produce an application in Delphi, which is saved as a **Project**:

* As you start up Delphi, a new Project opens

* Place components on the form (in the Form Designer)

* Give components meaningful names (in the Object Inspector)

* Arrange them the way you want the user interface to appear.

* Set properties of your components (in the Object Inspector)

* Create event handlers (the procedures that make your application run) in the Code Editor

As you design the user interface in the **Form Designer**, Delphi generates the underlying Object Pascal code. When you modify properties of components, Delphi changes the source files. You can add code to the source files yourself using the Code Editor.

DO NOT change any of the code Delphi creates. If you want to change the name of a component, you must do this in the Object Inspector. If you change your mind and delete a component, you need only delete the component from the form and delete the code **within** its event-handler(s). Delphi will clear up the rest.

This is the code already generated for a new project:

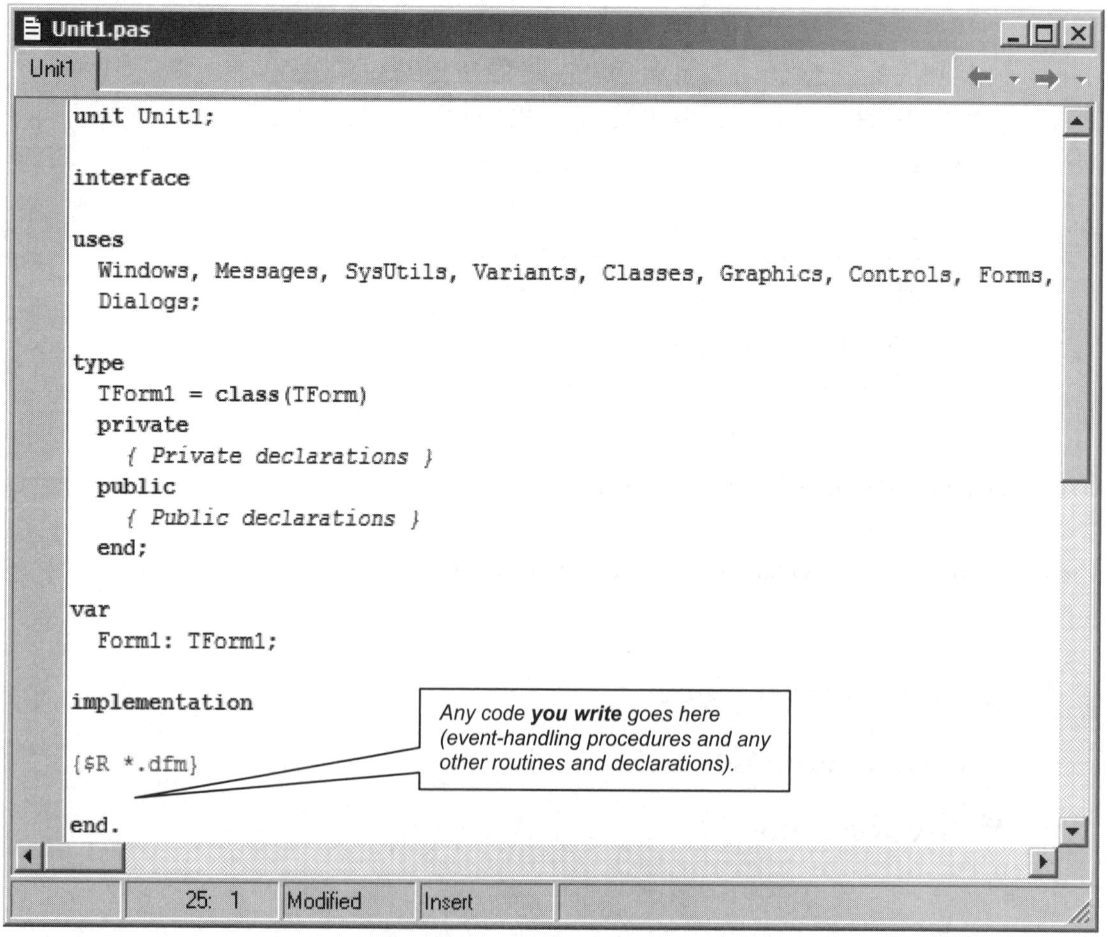

```
unit Unit1;

interface

uses
  Windows, Messages, SysUtils, Variants, Classes, Graphics, Controls, Forms,
  Dialogs;

type
  TForm1 = class(TForm)
  private
    { Private declarations }
  public
    { Public declarations }
  end;

var
  Form1: TForm1;

implementation

{$R *.dfm}

end.
```

*Any code **you write** goes here (event-handling procedures and any other routines and declarations).*

Figure 12.3: The Code Explorer window before any components have been added

Worked Example

The aim of this project is to display the message "Hello World" in English and Spanish ("Hola Mundo") on a form. The user will select the language to be displayed by clicking the appropriate button on the form. There is also a button to exit the project. An example of the finished form is shown below with labels indicating which components are used to create the form.

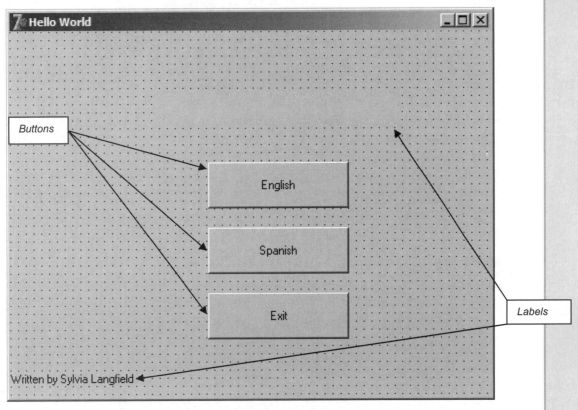

Figure 12.4: User Interface for 'Hello World' Project

This project has been designed so that you can practise the following activities:
- o Positioning and resizing a form on screen
- o Placing components on a form from the components page, moving and resizing them
- o Setting property values for form, label and button components at design time
- o Writing code in event-handling procedures to alter component property values at run time
- o Using the **Close** command to exit the application
- o Saving the form and the project on to disk.

Step 1 – Create the Interface

From the *Standard* Components palette,

- Double-click the **Button** component – this adds a button to the form
  (or single-click and click-and-drag across a diagonal on the form).

- Repeat this two more times.

- Double-click the **Label** component twice.

- Arrange the components as in Figure 12.4 by dragging and resizing if necessary.

Step 2 – Set the Properties

- Select the form in the Object Inspector. The list of properties includes **Caption** and **Name**.

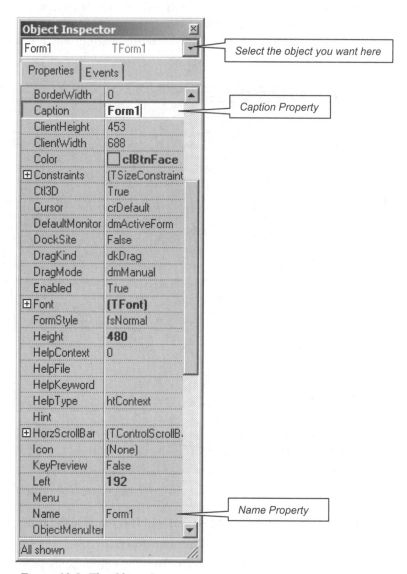

Figure 12.5: The Object Inspector

- Change the **Caption** property to *Hello World* – this will appear in the title bar.
- Change the **Name** property to *frmHello*.

Note: There are
many more
properties for each
component than
are listed. The ones
not mentioned
should be left at
their **default**
values.

- Now select each button and label in turn and set the property values as listed in the table below. Press the **Enter** key after each value, or your setting may not be saved.

Component	Property	Value
Button1	Name	btnEnglish
	Caption	English
Button2	Name	btnSpanish
	Caption	Spanish
Button3	Name	btnExit
	Caption	Exit
Label1	Name	lblMessage
	Caption	(leave blank)
	Alignment	taCenter
	Font	MS Sans Serif - Size 24 (click **...**)
Label 2	Name	lblAuthor
	Caption	Written by [your name]
	Font	MS Sans Serif - Size 8

> **Note:** Any properties that have been changed from their default are shown in bold in the Object Inspector (in Delphi 7 only).

Step 3 – Write the Code

One of the main strengths of a programming language like Delphi is that there is no need to restrict the user in what order they must interact with the application. Each component can detect system events (e.g. mouse movements and clicks). The user can press any button at any time and the program will respond accordingly. This is achieved by attaching the code to components and system events. It is therefore essential that the programmer knows exactly what they want to happen whenever any event occurs, a mouse-click on a button for example. It is the job of the programmer to write the instructions of what that component is to do when it detects particular system messages. This is done by writing code in the **Code Editor** window.

Properties are changed at run-time by assigning the new value in the code as follows:

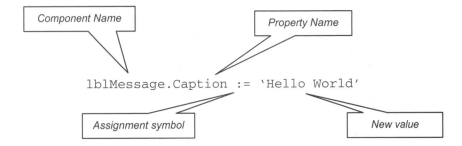

To write the code that should run when the user clicks on a button, double-click on the button and Delphi will provide you with the event-handler procedure template for the button's *OnClick* event. All code is placed between the **begin** and **end** after the procedure heading.

As you start typing the code, you will see Delphi provides you with help:

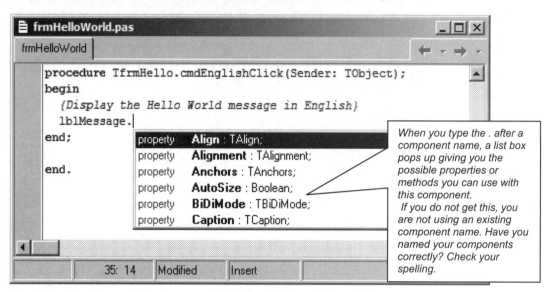

Figure 12.6: AutoComplete in action for objects

To toggle between form and unit, click on the **Toggle Form/Unit** button.

*   Double-click on each button in turn and write the necessary code.

Saving your form and project:

*   Pull down the **File** menu and select **Save All**.

*   You must now navigate your way to the your **Delphi Projects** folder and create a *Project1* folder.

*   Delphi asks you firstly to save the Form/Unit. Save it as *frmHelloWorld.pas*

*   You are now asked to save the project. Save it as *HelloProject.dpr*

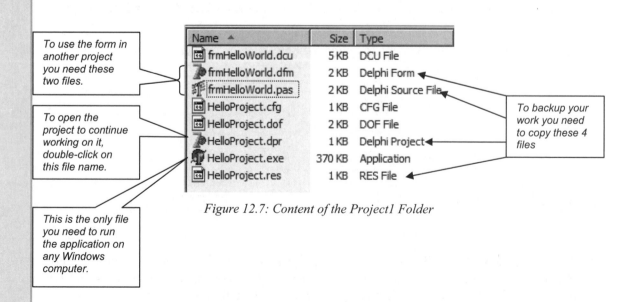

Figure 12.7: Content of the Project1 Folder

Running your application:

- Now compile and run the program by clicking on the **Run** button .

If you have made a mistake the compiler will give you an error message at the bottom of the window:

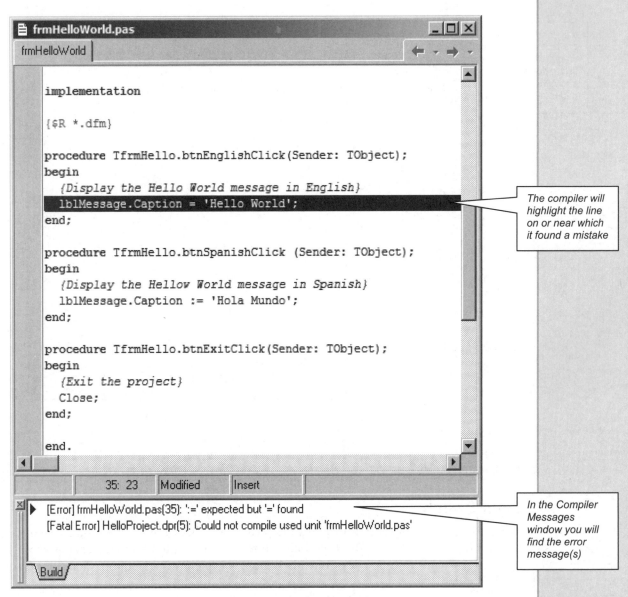

Figure 12.8: Compiler messages during compilation

- Go back into your code and edit any errors until the program will run. Test that all buttons work successfully.
- To stop any program, you can click the **Close** button.

Here is a complete list of the code you should have:

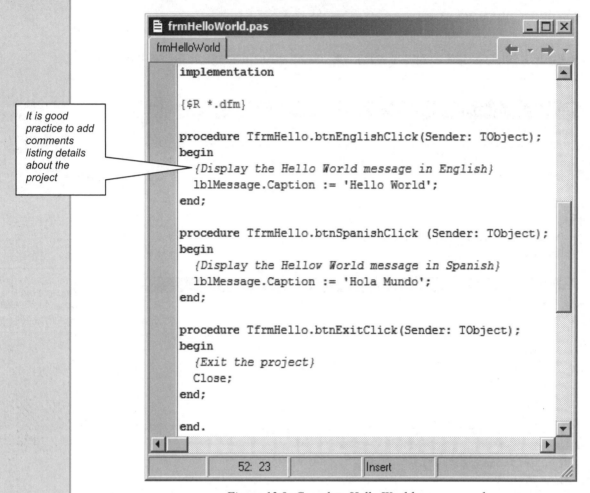

It is good practice to add comments listing details about the project

```
implementation

{$R *.dfm}

procedure TfrmHello.btnEnglishClick(Sender: TObject);
begin
  {Display the Hello World message in English}
  lblMessage.Caption := 'Hello World';
end;

procedure TfrmHello.btnSpanishClick (Sender: TObject);
begin
  {Display the Hellow World message in Spanish}
  lblMessage.Caption := 'Hola Mundo';
end;

procedure TfrmHello.btnExitClick(Sender: TObject);
begin
  {Exit the project}
  Close;
end;

end.
```

Figure 12.9: Complete Hello World program code

Exercise 12.1

Light Switch

When the application starts it displays the picture of a light bulb. When the user clicks on the button *'Turn the light on'*, the light bulb shines and the button message changes to *'Turn the light off'*. When the user clicks on this button, the picture and button should revert to their original states.

Step 1 – Create the Interface

- Set up the interface as below:

    (Once you have written and tested the code, align the buttons so that they are both on top of one another and the image components likewise.)

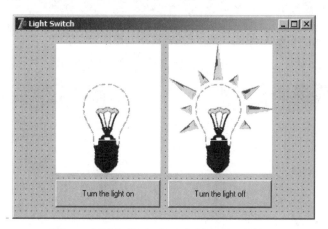

Figure 12.10: Light Switch User Interface

Step 2 – Set the Properties

- Change the properties of the components as shown in the table below:

Control	Property	Setting
Form1	Name	frmLightBulb
	Caption	Light Switch
Label1	Name	lblProgrammer
	Caption	Programmer: [your name]
Button1	Name	btnSwitchOn
	Caption	Switch the Light On
Button2	Name	btnSwitchOff
	Caption	Switch the Light Off
Image1	Name	imgLightOff
	Visible	True
	Picture	[image of a light bulb]
Image2	Name	imgLightOn
	Visible	False
	Picture	[image of a lightbulb]

Step 3 – Write the code

- Double-click on *btnSwitchOn* and write the code to hide *imgLightOff*:

```
imgLightOff.Visible := False
```

What code do you need to write to show *imgLightOn*?

You also want to hide *btnSwitchOn* and show *btnSwitchOff*. Add those statements.

- Now double-click on *btnSwitchOff* and write the code to:
    Show *btnSwitchOn*
    Hide *btnSwitchOff*
    Show *imgLightOff*
    Hide *imgLightOn*.

Your application should now switch
from this …   to this

Figure 12.11: Light off

Figure 12.12: Light on

and back again.

Exercise 12.2

Greetings

- Create the interface shown below.

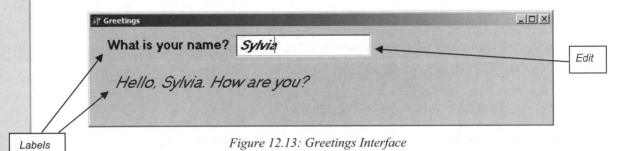

Figure 12.13: Greetings Interface

- Set the component properties as shown in the table:

Control	Property	Setting
Form1	Name	frmGreetings
	Caption	Greetings
Label1	Name	lblQuestion
	Caption	What is your name?
Edit1	Name	edtName
	Text	(blank)
Label2	Name	lblMessage
	Caption	(blank)

- Double-click on the **Edit** component. This will open the template for the event-handler procedure for the *OnChange* event of the **Edit** component. Add the line:

```
lblMessage.Caption := 'Hello, ' + edtName.Text + '. How are you?'
```

- Now test your program.

Exercise 12.3

List of Names

This program allows the user to add a name to the list box on the left by typing it into the edit box in the top right corner. **Clear** will clear all names out of the list box. A name selected in the list box can be deleted with the **Delete** button.

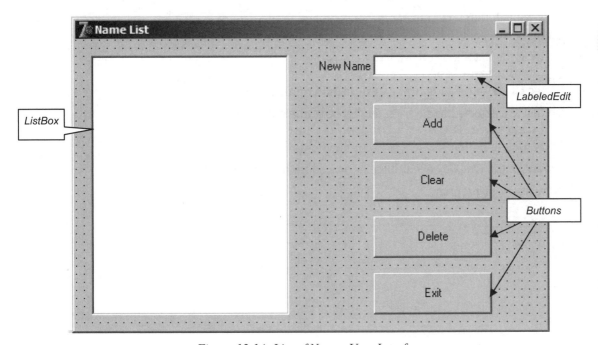

Figure 12.14: List of Names User Interface

- Create the user interface shown above.

- Set the component properties as shown in the table:

Control	Property	Setting
Form1	Name	frmNames
	Caption	Name List
ListBox1	Name	lboNames
	Sorted	True
LabeledEdit1	Name	ledtName
	Text	(blank)
	LabelPosition	lpLeft
	EditLabel.Caption *(Click the '+' next to EditLabel to view its subproperties)*	New Name
Button1	Name	btnAdd
	Caption	Add
Button2	Name	btnClear
	Caption	Clear
Button3	Name	btnDelete
	Caption	Delete
Button4	Name	btnExit
	Caption	Exit

- Double-click on the **Add** button. Insert the line:

```
lboNames.Items.Add (ledtName.Text)
```

  This will add the text in the *ledtName* edit box to the list box on the left. Because the **Sorted** property was set to *True*, the names will automatically be in alphabetical order.

- To clear the listbox insert the line

```
lboNames.Clear
```

  in the **Clear** button's *OnClick* event-handler procedure.

- To delete a selected name from the list box, insert the line

```
lboNames.DeleteSelected
```

  in the **Delete** button's *OnClick* event-handler procedure.

- Complete the *OnClick* event-handler procedure for the **Exit** button.

- Now test your program.

Exercises

12.4 Write a program that shows different messages in a label depending on which button is pressed. The buttons have captions *Message 1*, *Message 2* and *Message 3*.

12.5 Find 3 different images and place them on a form. Write event-handlers for 3 buttons that control which image is visible.

12.6 Adapt the program from Exercise 12.2, providing two edit boxes where the user can type in their first name into one edit box and their surname into the other edit box. When a button is pressed, the message should incorporate the full name.

Summary

You have learnt to:

- ✓ place components on a form
- ✓ set properties of components in the **Object Inspector**
- ✓ write event-handlers in procedure templates provided by Delphi when double-clicking a component
- ✓ set properties at run-time using assignment statements of the form

  ```
  ComponentName.Property := PropertyValue
  ```

- ✓ save form and project in a folder for that application
- ✓ compile and run a program
- ✓ use the **Close** statement to exit the application
- ✓ concatenate strings using the + operator
- ✓ use the following components, properties, events and methods

Component	Properties	Event	Method
Form	Name, Caption		
Button	Name, Caption	Click	
Label	Name, Caption, Alignment, Font		
Image	Name, Picture, Visible		
Edit	Name, Text	Change	
ListBox	Name, Sorted		Clear, DeleteSelected, Items.Add
LabeledEdit	Name, Text, LabelPosition, EditLabel.Caption		

Chapter 13 – Selection

Exercise 13.1

This program lets the user choose a number from a combo box and displays a message in a separate message box as to whether it was the lucky number or not.

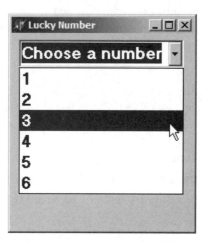

Figure 13.1: Choosing one option from a combo box

Gives this   or this message

Figure 13.2   *Figure 13.3*

- Set up the user interface with the following component properties:

Component	Property	Setting
Form1	Name	frmLuckyNumber
	Caption	Lucky Number
ComboBox1	Name	cboNumber
	Text	Choose a number
	Font	Bold 14
	Items	1
		2
		3
		4
		5
		6

- Now double-click on the combo box to get the template for its *OnChange* event-handler.

- Add the following code:
  ```
  if cboNumber.ItemIndex = 5  // ItemIndex starts at 0
      then ShowMessage ('Jackpot')
      else ShowMessage ('No luck this time')
  ```

- Now test your program.

Later on, you could develop this program so that the lucky number changes each time the program is run

Exercise 13.2

Change the *Light Switch* application from Exercise 12.2, so you only use one button (name it btnSwitch). Instead of hiding and showing the buttons, change the caption on the button. The button-click event now needs to check the value of the Boolean variable *LightOn*.

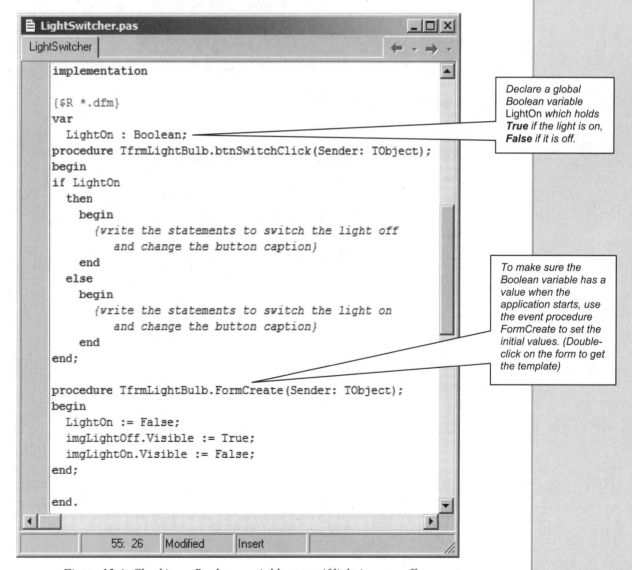

Figure 13.4: Checking a Boolean variable to see if light is on or off

Exercise 13.3

The user is presented with two sets of radio buttons to choose the type of shape to be displayed and what colour the shape should be.

Step 1 – Create the Interface

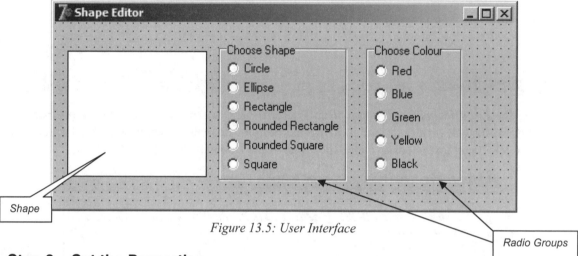

Figure 13.5: User Interface

Step 2 – Set the Properties

Component	Property	Setting
Form1	Name	frmShapes
	Caption	Shape Editor
Shape1	Name	shpShape
	Shape	stRectangle
	Brush.Color	clRed
RadioGroup1	Name	rgrpShape
	Caption	Choose Shape
	Items	Circle
		Ellipse
		Rectangle
		Rounded Rectangle
		Rounded Square
		Square
	ItemIndex	2
RadioGroup2	Name	rgrpColour
	Caption	Choose Colour
	Items	Red
		Blue
		Green
		Yellow
		Black
	ItemIndex	0

Step 3 – Write the code

- Double-click on **rgrpShape** and write the code for choosing the shape:

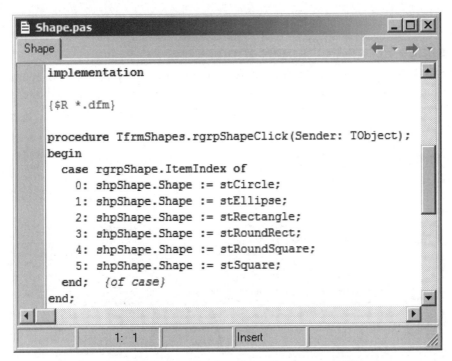

```
implementation

{$R *.dfm}

procedure TfrmShapes.rgrpShapeClick(Sender: TObject);
begin
  case rgrpShape.ItemIndex of
    0: shpShape.Shape := stCircle;
    1: shpShape.Shape := stEllipse;
    2: shpShape.Shape := stRectangle;
    3: shpShape.Shape := stRoundRect;
    4: shpShape.Shape := stRoundSquare;
    5: shpShape.Shape := stSquare;
  end;   {of case}
end;
```

*Figure 13.6: Event procedure for radio group **rgrpShape***

> **Note:** Always let Delphi provide you with the template for the event handler by double-clicking on the component or selecting the appropriate event from the Object Inspector.

Delphi provides system constants for basic colours such as *clBlue*. To fill a shape with a colour, use the property **Brush.Color**.

- Double-click on *rgrpColour* and write the code to change the colourfill of the shape. For example, to fill the shape with the colour blue, write:

```
shpShape.Brush.Color := clBlue
```

- Test your program thoroughly.

Exercise 13.4

The Message Formatter Application

The aim of the *Message Formatter* application is for a user to enter a short message into the edit box. Then they select colour and styles using the radio buttons and check boxes. When the **Format Message** button is pressed the message is formatted as required. The **Exit** button terminates the application.

Step 1 – Create the Interface

Set up the user interface as below:

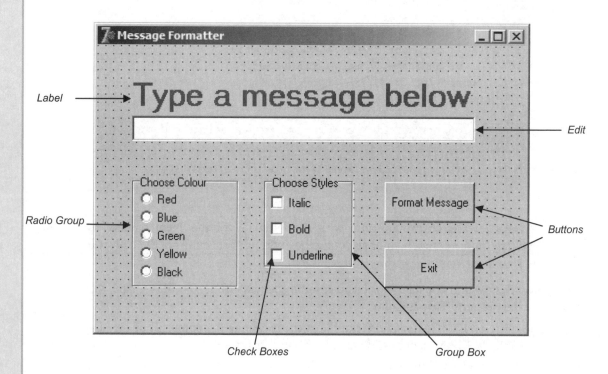

Figure 13.7: The Message Formatter user interface

Step 2 – Set the Properties

Change the properties of the components as shown in the table below:

Component	Property	Setting
Form1	Name	frmMessageFormatter
	Caption	Message Formatter
Label1	Name	lblMessage
	Caption	Type a message below
Edit1	Name	edtMessage
	Text	(blank)
RadioGroup1	Name	rgrpColour
	Caption	Choose Colour
	Items	Red
		Blue
		Green
		Yellow
		Black
	ItemIndex	4
GroupBox1	Name	grpStyle
	Caption	Choose Style
Checkbox1	Name	chkItalic
	Caption	Italic
Checkbox2	Name	chkBold
	Caption	Bold
Checkbox3	Name	chkUnderline
	Caption	Underline
Button1	Name	btnFormat
	Caption	Format Message
Button2	Name	btnExit
	Caption	Exit

Step 3 – Write the code

Double-click on the **Exit** button and write the code to close the application.

Double-click on the **Format Message** button and write the code to change the colour. When this works correctly, add the code to change the style.

Note that styles are set as a list:
```
edtMessage.Font.Style := [fsBold, fsUnderline, fsItalic]
```
will set all these styles.
```
edtMessage.Font.Style := []; {empty list}
```
will clear all styles.

If you want to add bold style to whatever is there already:
```
edtMessage.Font.Style := edtMessage.Font.Style + [fsBold]
```

Test that your program works for all combinations of colour and style choices.

Exercise 13.5

Password Entry

Write a password entry program. The program should check the entered password when a button is pressed, and should allow three attempts at entering the correct password. If the password is incorrect, the user can try again. After three unsuccessful attempts, a message will appear, telling the user they have failed to enter the system. The program should disable any further attempts at entering a password.

Hints:

Use the **MaskEdit** component in the **Additional** Component palette. The **PasswordChar** property can be set to the character to be displayed when the user types a password into the edit box to keep the password secret.

Passwords should only consist of alphanumeric characters. The **EditMask** property lets you define a mask to allow only alphanumeric characters. Setting **EditMask** to *aaaaaaaa* will allow up to 8 alphanumeric characters to be entered. For a full list of codes to set masks, see Delphi Help: **TEditMask type**.

Declare a global integer variable to keep a check on how many attempts have been made at entering the password.

Instead of using the *ShowMessage* procedure, you could try the *MessageDlg* function.

For example

```
if MessageDlg ('Wrong password! Try again?',
               mtConfirmation,[mbYes, mbNo],0)= mrNo
   then Close // exit the application
```

will show this message dialog:

Figure 13.8: Confirmation dialog window

The message box returns the values *mrYes* or *mrNo* depending on which button is clicked.

You can try message type *mtWarning* or *mtError* instead of *mtConfirmation*.

[*mbYes, mbNo*] is the list of message buttons to be shown in the dialog window. Other buttons available are: *mbOK, mbCancel, mbAbort, mbRetry, mbIgnore, mbAll, mbHelp*.

Exercise 13.6

Extend the Message Formatter application, so the user can also choose the size of the font.

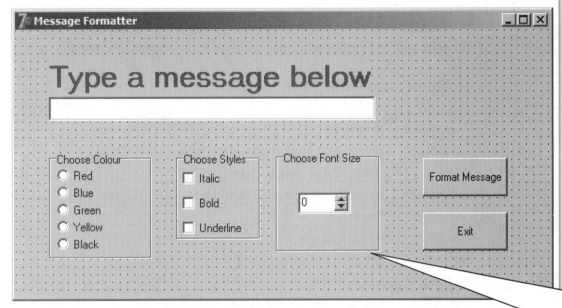

Figure 13.9: Message Formatter with Font Size Selection

GroupBox with SpinEdit (from the Samples Component Palette). Make sure the GroupBox is selected when placing the SpinEdit into it.

- Add the following line into the btnFormat's *OnClick* event-handler.

```
edtMessage.Font.Size := sedtFontSize.Value
```

Edit box

SpinEdit

Property that stores the number selected

Summary

You have learnt to:

- ✓ declare global (unit wide) variables at the top of the **implementation** section
- ✓ use the **if** statement
- ✓ use the **case** statement
- ✓ use the *ShowMessage* procedure to display a message in a separate window
- ✓ use the *MessageDlg* function to display a message in a customised window with reply buttons
- ✓ use the following components, properties and events

Component	Properties	Event
ComboBox	Name, Text, Font, Items, ItemIndex	Change
Shape	Name, Shape, Brush.Color	
RadioGroup	Name, Caption, Items, ItemIndex	Click
GroupBox	Name, Caption	
CheckBox	Name, Caption	
Edit	Name, Font.Color, Font.Style, Font.Size	
SpinEdit	Name, Value	
MaskEdit	Name, Text, PasswordChar, EditMask	

Chapter 14 – Iteration

Exercise 14.1

- Write a program that shows a message 5 times, and then shows a good-bye message:

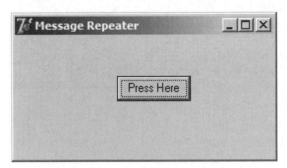

Figure 14.1: Message Repeater

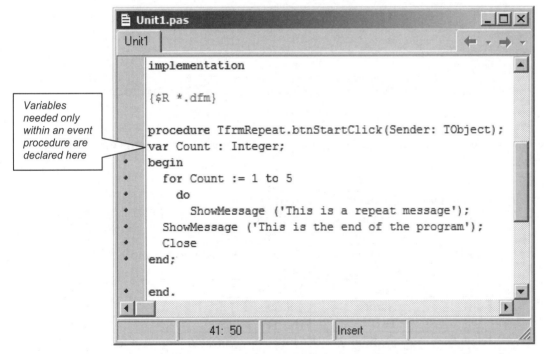

Variables needed only within an event procedure are declared here

```
implementation

{$R *.dfm}

procedure TfrmRepeat.btnStartClick(Sender: TObject);
var Count : Integer;
begin
   for Count := 1 to 5
     do
        ShowMessage ('This is a repeat message');
   ShowMessage ('This is the end of the program');
   Close
end;

end.
```

*Figure 14.2: Code for **Press Here** button*

Exercise 14.2

- Adapt the program from Exercise 14.1 above, so that the user can choose how many times the message should be repeated with the aid of a **SpinEdit** component.

Exercise 14.3

In this application the user types a message into the **Edit** box and selects a number from the **SpinEdit** component and this is the number of times the message is displayed in the **Memo** component.

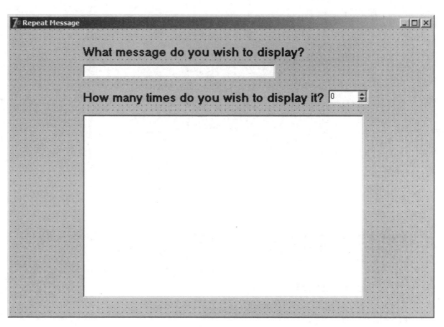

Figure 14.3: Repeat Message User Interface

- Set up the above user interface and change the properties of the components as follows:

Component	Property	Setting
Form1	Name	frmRepeat
	Caption	Repeat Message
Label1	Caption	What message do you wish to display?
	Font	Bold 14
Edit1	Name	edtText
	Text	(blank)
Label2	Caption	How many times do you wish to display it?
	Font	Bold 14
SpinEdit1	Name	sedtNumber
	MaxValue	20
Memo1	Name	memText
	Enabled	False
	Lines	(blank)

- Double-click on the **SpinEdit** component and type the following code into the event procedure template:

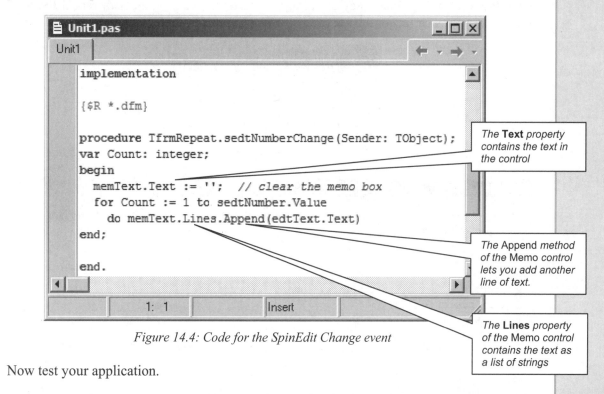

```pascal
implementation

{$R *.dfm}

procedure TfrmRepeat.sedtNumberChange(Sender: TObject);
var Count: integer;
begin
  memText.Text := '';   // clear the memo box
  for Count := 1 to sedtNumber.Value
    do memText.Lines.Append(edtText.Text)
end;

end.
```

*The **Text** property contains the text in the control*

The Append method of the Memo control lets you add another line of text.

*The **Lines** property of the Memo control contains the text as a list of strings*

Figure 14.4: Code for the SpinEdit Change event

- Now test your application.

Exercise 14.4

- Adapt the program from Exercise 14.3 above, to produce a triangle of symbols chosen by the user

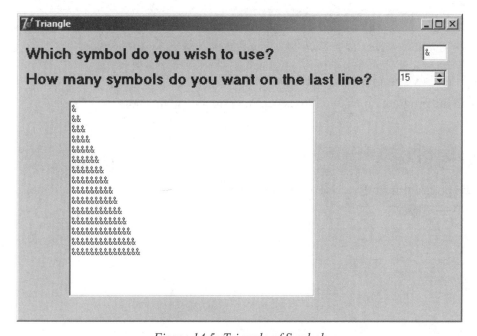

Figure 14.5: Triangle of Symbols

Exercise 14.5

When the user presses **Play**, they are asked a question. The program will repeat the question until the answer is correct or the user does not type anything into the input box.

Figure 14.6: Guessing game User Interface

```
implementation

{$R *.dfm}

procedure TForm1.btnPlayClick(Sender: TObject);
var Answer: String;
begin
  repeat
    Answer := InputBox('Guessing Game', 'Who invented the first computer?','');
  until (Answer = 'Babbage') or (Answer = '');
  if Answer = ''
    then ShowMessage ('It was Charles Babbage')
    else ShowMessage ('Well Done');
  Close;
end;

end.
```

Figure 14.7: Code to repeat the question using an InputBox

- Copy the above program and test it thoroughly.
- Extend the program, to enable it to accept incorrect capitalisation.

Exercise 14.6

Adapt the program from Exercise 14.5 above, so the user will be asked a maximum of 5 times for the correct answer.

Exercise 14.7

Balloon Flight

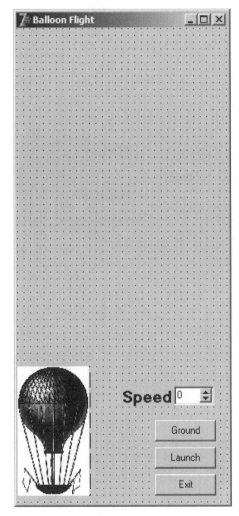

Figure 14.8: Balloon Launcher

- Set up the user interface as shown with an image of a balloon at the bottom of the page.

- Set **MaxValue** and **MinValue** properties of the **SpinEdit** component so that the user can only select a value between 0 and 10.

- Write the code to do the following:

  Clicking the **Ground** button should return the balloon to its starting position (set its **Top** property).

  Clicking the **Launch** button should repeatedly decrement the balloon's **Top** property by the number selected in the **SpinEdit** component until the balloon has reached the top of the form. (**Top** <= 0).

  Clicking on **Exit**, closes the application.

- Test your program.

You will find that the balloon reaches the top in an instant rather than slowly floating up.

Another way of implementing repeated actions is by introducing a timer.

- Remove the code in the **Launch** button's *OnClick* event handler.

- Add a **Timer** (from the **System** Component palette) to the form. As the timer is invisible during the running of the application, it does not matter where it is placed.

Note: You can download this picture from *www.payne-gallway.co.uk*

- Set the timer's **Interval** property to *100* and its **Enabled** property to *False*. Each unit of time is 1 millisecond, so the timer's interval is 0.1 second.

- Enable the timer when the **Launch** button is pressed. The following code in the timer's *Timer* event-handler will be executed after each interval of 0.1 second.

```
imgBalloon.Top := imgBalloon.Top - sedtSpeed.Value;
if imgBalloon.Top <= 0  // test for top of form
   then tmrBalloon.Enabled := False; // disable timer
```

- Find a way of preventing further clicks of the **Launch** button from driving the balloon off the top of the form.

Summary

You have learnt to:

- ✓ declare local variables within an event procedure
- ✓ use a **for** loop in an event procedure
- ✓ use a **repeat** loop in an event procedure
- ✓ use the **InputBox** function to get user input
- ✓ use the following components, properties and events

Component	Properties	Event	Method
SpinEdit	MaxValue	Change	
Memo	Name, Enabled, Text, Lines		Append
Timer	Name, Interval, Enabled	Timer	
Image	Top		

Chapter 15 – Functions

When a user types a number into an **Edit** box, Delphi treats it as text. Before we can use this input as a number we need to convert it into a number. Similarly, if we want to display the result of a calculation in a component, we need to convert a numeric result into a string. Delphi supplies built-in functions for this:

Function	Returns
IntToStr(*Integer-type value*)	A **string** representation of the integer supplied
StrToInt(*String-type value*)	The **integer** equivalent of the string supplied
FloatToStr(*Real-type value*)	A **string** representation of the real number supplied
StrToFloat(*String-type value*)	The **real** equivalent of the string supplied

Of course we can also use the built-in functions we met in chapter 6.

Exercise 15.1

- Create the user interface for this simple adding machine:

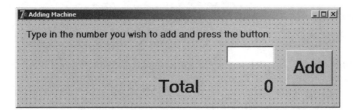

Figure 15.1: A simple Adding Machine

- Set the properties:

Component	Property	Setting
Form1	Name	frmAddingMachine
	Caption	Adding Machine
Label1	Caption	Type the number you wish to add and press the button
	Font	Bold 12
Edit1	Name	edtNumber
	Text	(blank)
Label2	Caption	Total
	Font	Bold 24
Label3	Name	lblResult
	Caption	0
	Font	Bold 24
	Alignment	taRightJustify
Button1	Name	btnAdd
	Font	Bold 24
	Caption	Add

- Double-click on the button control and add the following code:

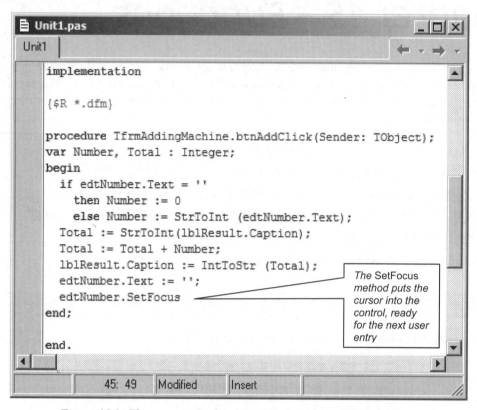

```
implementation

{$R *.dfm}

procedure TfrmAddingMachine.btnAddClick(Sender: TObject);
var Number, Total : Integer;
begin
  if edtNumber.Text = ''
    then Number := 0
    else Number := StrToInt (edtNumber.Text);
  Total := StrToInt(lblResult.Caption);
  Total := Total + Number;
  lblResult.Caption := IntToStr (Total);
  edtNumber.Text := '';
  edtNumber.SetFocus
end;

end.
```

The SetFocus method puts the cursor into the control, ready for the next user entry

Figure 15.2: The event procedure to add a number to the Totals box

Exercise 15.2

- Set up the user interface to show the Times Table for the selected number.

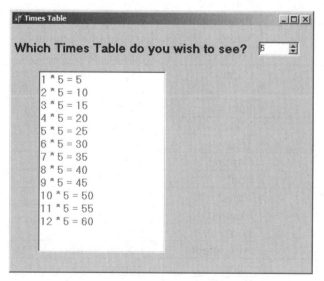

Figure 15.3: The Times Table application

- Write the code for the **SpinEdit** *Change* event to show the display in a **Memo** box.

Exercise 15.3

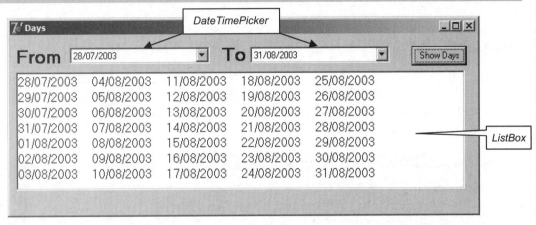

Figure 15.4: User Interface to show days between two chosen dates

- Create the user interface as above.
- Set the properties:

Component	Property	Setting
Label1	Caption	From
DateTimePicker1	Name	dtpFrom
Label2	Caption	To
DateTimePicker2	Name	dtpTo
Button1	Name	btnShow
	Caption	Show Days
ListBox1	Name	lboDays
	Font.Size	12
	Columns	6
	Height	160
	Width	600

- Write the code for the button's *OnClick* event-handler as follows:

```
var Day: TDateTime;
begin
  lboDays.Clear; // make sure list box is empty
  Day := dtpFrom.Date; // get first date
  while Day < dtpTo.Date
    do
      begin
        lboDays.Items.Add(DateToStr(Day));
        Day := Day + 1; // move to next date
      end;
end;
```

> This function changes the date to a string to be displayed in the listbox

- Test your program.

Exercise 15.4

- Create the user interface below and write the code to generate a random amount between 1p and £2 when the button **New Selection** is pressed. The user enters the amount inserted as coins into the edit box and when **Calculate Change** is pressed, the program shows the amount of change due.

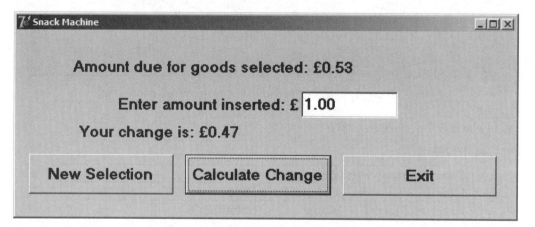

Figure 15.5: Snack Machine User Interface

If not enough money was inserted a message should alert the user:

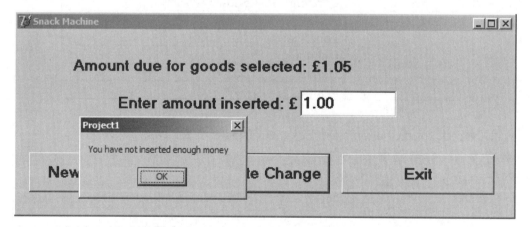

Figure 15.6: Error message if not enough money inserted

Exercise 15.5

- Create a user interface for a program that shows the amount collected from fund raising next to the top of the bar gauge.

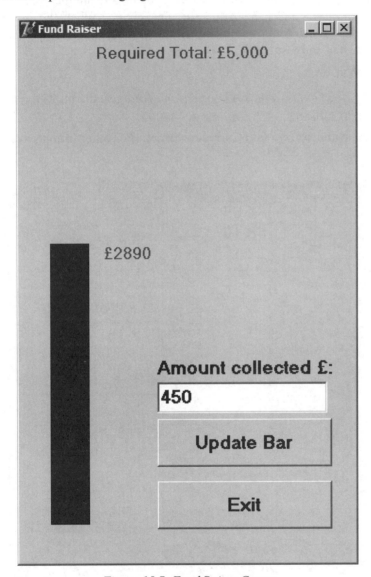

Figure 15.7: Fund Raiser Gauge

- Write the code to add amounts typed in by the user to a running total. The bar should adjust in size in proportion to the amount of money collected so far. When the required total has been reached, the program should display a message.

  Hint: Use a **Shape** component for the bar. Set its **Height** to *0* and **Top** to *550* at design-time. The code should increase the height of the bar in proportion to the running total and then change the **Top** property to *500*-**Height**. The maximum height will be 500 units.

- Test your program.

Exercise 15.6

- Create a user interface for a program that allows a user to create a list of prices for goods sold. The running *GoodsTotal* should be updated and another item added to the list each time the user clicks the **AddToInvoice** button. When the user clicks the **Total** button, the *GoodsTotal* should be displayed and the *VAT* and *InvoiceTotal* should be calculated and displayed.

- Test your program.

  Hint: To display the *GoodsTotal*, *VAT* and *InvoiceTotal* use the built-in function:

  ```
  FloatToStrF (Total, ffCurrency, 5, 2)
  ```

  This formats the number *Total* into Currency format. (For other formats available see Delphi Help.)

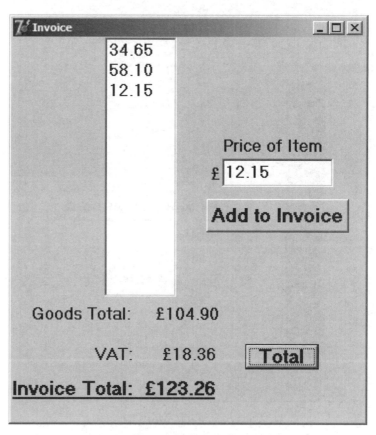

Figure 15.8: Invoice

User-defined functions

Just as in a console application, we can write our own function definitions:

```
{$R *.dfm}

uses StrUtils;

function IsPalindrome (S: String) : Boolean;
begin
  Result := (S = ReverseString(S) )  // comparison in brackets yields
end;                                 // Boolean result

procedure TfrmPalindromeTester.edtWordChange(Sender: TObject);
begin
  if IsPalindrome (edtWord.Text)
    then
      lblMessage.Caption := 'This is a Palindrome'
    else
      lblMessage.Caption := 'Not a Palindrome'
end;

end.
```

Any units you are using are declared here.
Your declarations of constants, variables and functions go after this line.

45: 30   Insert

Figure 15.9: Declaring and using a Boolean function

Exercise 15.7

- Make a user interface as shown below and copy the above code.
- Remember to add the **StrUtils** unit to the **uses** clause.

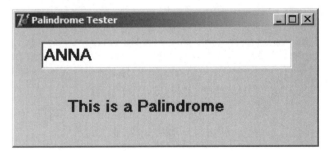

Figure 15.10: Palindrome Tester application

- Test your program.
- Try some other palindromes like: 'evil rats on no star live'.
- Modify the program to accept assymmetrical capitalisation of the text entered.

Hint: *Use an initialised local variable to store the largest number so far.*

Exercise 15.8

Design a user interface and write the necessary code to display 6 random numbers between 1 and 10 in a list box and put the largest of these numbers into a separate edit box.

Summary

You have learnt to:

✓ use built-in functions

✓ declare required units in a **uses** clause

✓ define and use your own functions

✓ use the following components, properties and methods

Component	Properties	Method
Edit		SetFocus
DateTimePicker	Date	
Label	Alignment	
ListBox	Font.Size, Columns, Height, Width	

Chapter 16 – Arrays

Although we can display items in list boxes or memo boxes, we sometimes want to store items not for display or of a type other than *String*.

One-Dimensional Arrays

Exercise 16.1

A program is to display a list of item descriptions. When a user selects an item, its unit price is displayed.

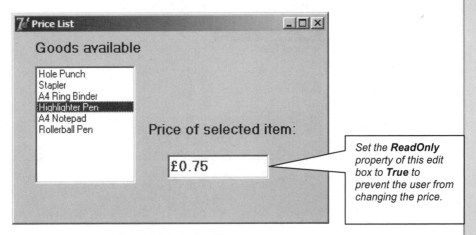

Figure 16.1: Price List

- Create the user interface as above. In the *FormCreate* event-handler, assign the following item descriptions and prices to elements of two arrays *Item* and *Price* respectively.

  ```
  Item[0] := 'Hole Punch';        Price[0] := 2.95;
  Item[1] := 'Stapler';           Price[1] := 3.50;
  Item[2] := 'A4 Ring Binder';    Price[2] := 1.50;
  Item[3] := 'Highlighter Pen';   Price[3] := 0.75;
  Item[4] := 'A4 Notepad';        Price[4] := 1.20;
  Item[5] := 'Rollerball Pen';    Price[5] := 0.95;
  ```

- Then populate a list box with the item descriptions:

  ```
  for Count := 0 to 5
    do
      lboItems.Items.Add(Item[Count])
  ```

- Now write the code to display the price for the selected item in the list box's *OnClick* event-handler. Remember that the **ItemIndex** property of the list box, which can be read at run-time, is also the array index of the item's price.

- Use the *FloatToStrF* function to display the price formatted as currency.

Exercise 16.2

Adapt your program from Exercise 16.1 to include a second list box **Order Form** in which the user can set up a list of items selected from the **Goods available** list. The **Total Price** edit box should automatically update to show the running total of the value of the items on the order form.

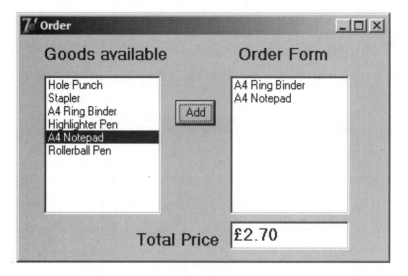

Figure 16.2: Order Form User Interface

Exercise 16.3

Write a program to test the user's knowledge of countries and their capital cities. One list box should contain the countries and another the capitals. The user selects a country from one list box and the corresponding capital from the other list box. When the button is pressed, the program will give either the message that the answer is correct, or the correct answer.

Hint: Show the content of the listboxes in alphabetical order.

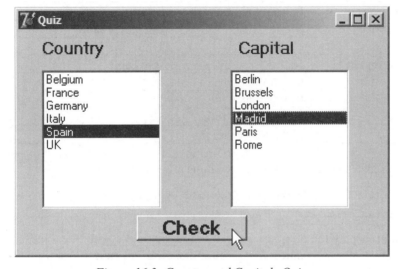

Figure 16.3: Country and Capitals Quiz

Exercise 16.4

Write a password entry program. Six user IDs and passwords are stored in 2 arrays. The user has to type in a user ID and a matching password. If the user has not entered the correct password after 3 attempts, the program should not allow the user any further attempts.

Figure 16.4: Password Entry

Two-Dimensional Arrays

The cells of the **StringGrid** component can be accessed like the elements of a two-dimensional array.

Exercise 16.5

Create a form with a string grid and set the following properties:

Component	Property	Setting
Form1	Name	frmTimesTable
	Caption	Times Table
StringGrid1	Name	sgrdTable
	ColCount	11
	RowCount	11
	DefaultColWidth	30
	DefaultRowHeight	24

Resize the string grid so that all rows and columns are visible.

The cells are addressed as in the example statement below:

```
sgrdTable.Cells[Column, Row] := IntToStr(Column * Row)
```

Write the code to display the numbers 1 to 10 in the row and column headings. The cells should display the product of row heading and column heading, making a look-up table for the times table:

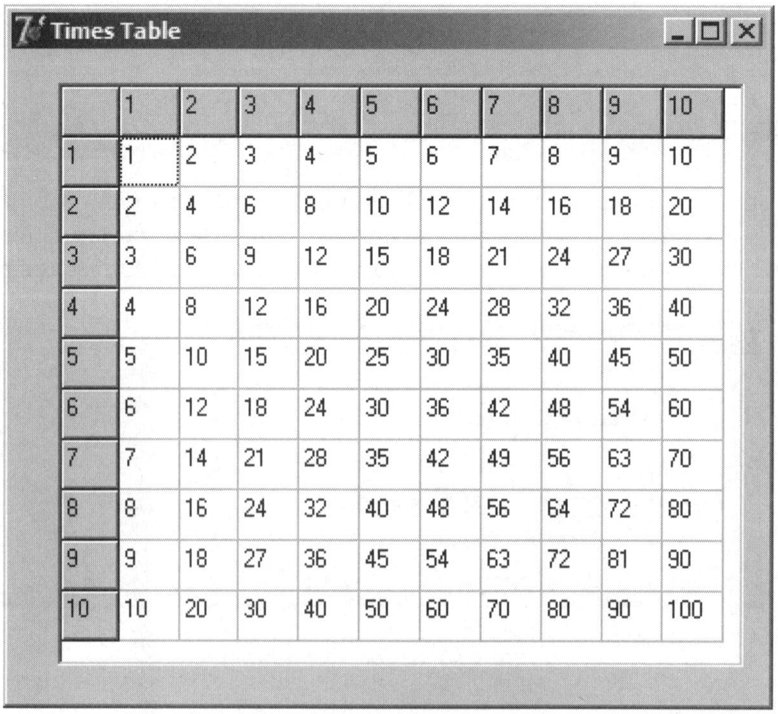

Figure 16.5: The Times Table grid

Exercise 16.6

The following program displays a timetable as organised in a certain college. Subjects are timetabled into blocks that occur at certain times in the week:

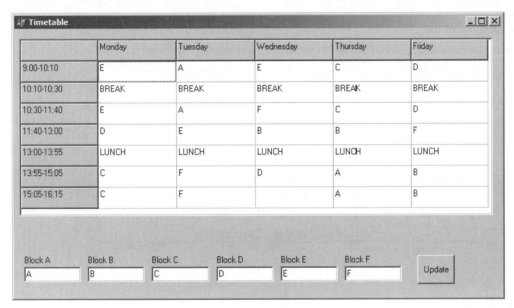

Figure 16.6: Timetable structure

When the user types in the subjects for each block and then clicks the **Update** button, the program automatically distributes the subjects into the correct lesson slots in the string grid:

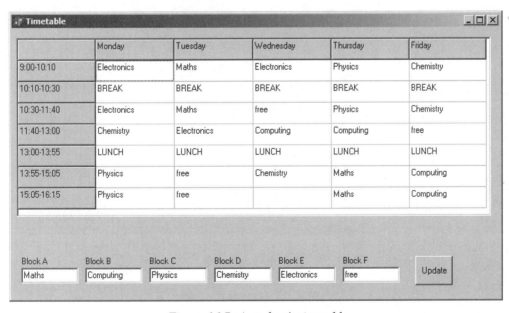

Figure 16.7: A student's timetable

- Make a timetable program to fit your school/college's timetable structure.
- Test it by typing your own subjects into the blocks and click the **Update** button.

Summary

You have learnt to:

- ✓ use one-dimensional arrays to store data not being displayed
- ✓ use string grids as two-dimensional arrays for display purposes
- ✓ use the following components and properties

Component	Properties
Edit	ReadOnly
StringGrid	ColCount, RowCount, DefaultColWidth, DefaultRowHeight
	Cells[ColIndex, RowIndex]

Chapter 17 – Procedures

User-Defined Procedures

Event-driven programming relies on the use of event-handling procedures. However, you may wish to write other routines to group statements together, either to make the code more transparent or to avoid repetitive code. Chapter 15 introduced user-defined functions into the event-driven programming environment. In the same way, the user can write user-defined procedures. Routine definitions which are to be available throughout a unit, are written after the implementation statement:

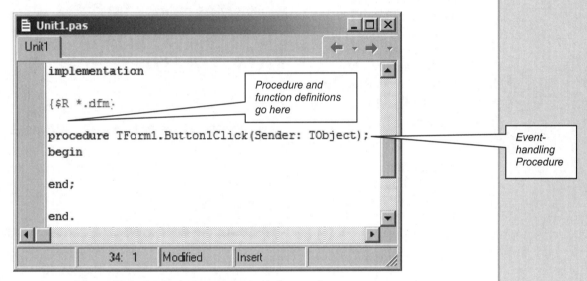

Figure 17.1: Implementation section of a new form

Every event procedure has a *Sender* parameter of type *TObject*.

Sender is a reference back to the object that initiated the event.

Parameters are very useful for user-defined functions and procedures, as they allow code to be reused with different parameters (see Chapter 8).

Exercise 17.1

The program is a basic model of a lift. The user can press a button on any floor and the lift will move to that floor.

When your program works, you may wish to improve the model to make it more realistic. You can give your lift doors that open on arrival, and close before departure. You can set up a radio group to indicate the current position of the lift. And so on…..

- Create a user interface as shown in Figure 17.2. Make the height of the lift an easy-to-use number, and evenly space the rectangular bars showing the floors.

- Name the form *frmLift*.

- Name the lift **shpLift**.

- Note down the values of the lift's **Top** property as you position it on each floor. You will need these later.

- Name the buttons consecutively **btn1**, **btn2** etc.

- Name the timers **tmrLiftUp** and **tmrLiftDown**. Their position is not important, as they are invisible during run-time.

- Set the timer intervals at 10 and disable the timers.

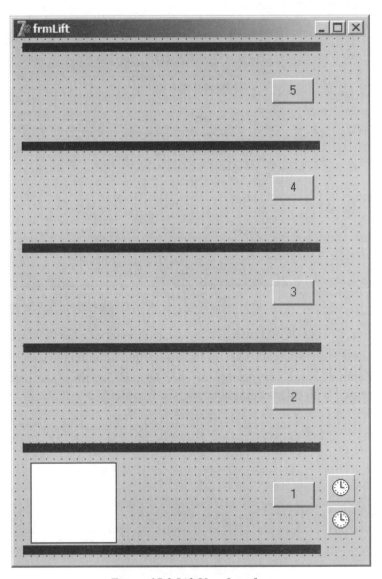

Figure 17.2 Lift User Interface

- Write the code as shown but remember to adjust the numbers for *Destination*, depending on what measurements you have noted down for the **Top** property of your lift.

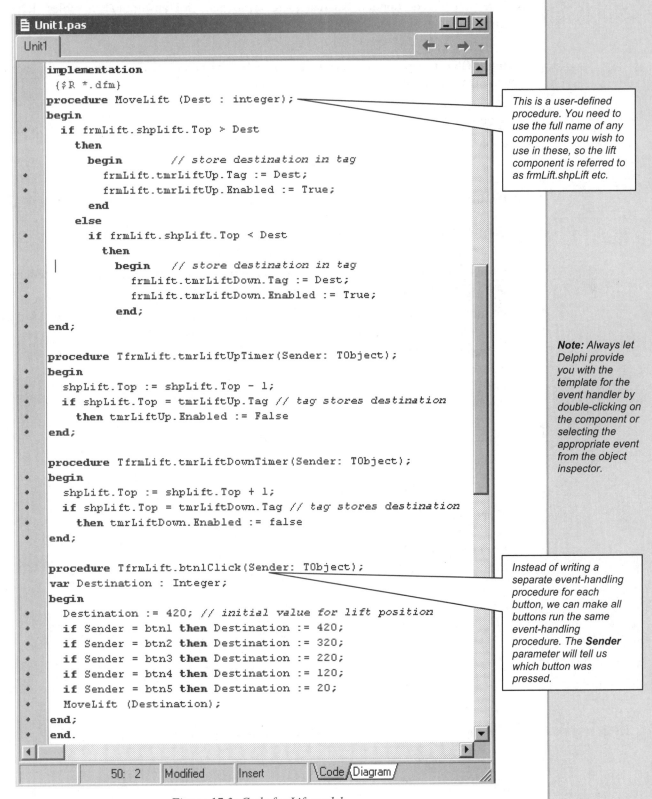

```
implementation
 {$R *.dfm}
procedure MoveLift (Dest : integer);
begin
  if frmLift.shpLift.Top > Dest
    then
      begin          // store destination in tag
        frmLift.tmrLiftUp.Tag := Dest;
        frmLift.tmrLiftUp.Enabled := True;
      end
    else
      if frmLift.shpLift.Top < Dest
        then
          begin    // store destination in tag
            frmLift.tmrLiftDown.Tag := Dest;
            frmLift.tmrLiftDown.Enabled := True;
          end;
end;

procedure TfrmLift.tmrLiftUpTimer(Sender: TObject);
begin
  shpLift.Top := shpLift.Top - 1;
  if shpLift.Top = tmrLiftUp.Tag // tag stores destination
    then tmrLiftUp.Enabled := False
end;

procedure TfrmLift.tmrLiftDownTimer(Sender: TObject);
begin
  shpLift.Top := shpLift.Top + 1;
  if shpLift.Top = tmrLiftDown.Tag // tag stores destination
    then tmrLiftDown.Enabled := false
end;

procedure TfrmLift.btn1Click(Sender: TObject);
var Destination : Integer;
begin
  Destination := 420; // initial value for lift position
  if Sender = btn1 then Destination := 420;
  if Sender = btn2 then Destination := 320;
  if Sender = btn3 then Destination := 220;
  if Sender = btn4 then Destination := 120;
  if Sender = btn5 then Destination := 20;
  MoveLift (Destination);
end;
end.
```

This is a user-defined procedure. You need to use the full name of any components you wish to use in these, so the lift component is referred to as frmLift.shpLift etc.

Note: Always let Delphi provide you with the template for the event handler by double-clicking on the component or selecting the appropriate event from the object inspector.

Instead of writing a separate event-handling procedure for each button, we can make all buttons run the same event-handling procedure. The **Sender** parameter will tell us which button was pressed.

Figure 17.3: Code for Lift model

Each component has a **Tag** property that has no predefined meaning. It is provided for the convenience of the programmer. It can be used for storing an additional integer value. Here it is used to store the destination, so that there is no need for any global variables. It is good programming to avoid global variables whenever possible.

- In the Object Inspector, choose the **Events** tab. In the *OnClick* drop-down box for each of the other buttons choose the *btn1Click* event.
- Now test your program.

Can you avoid the problem of a lift stalling when it is called while it is still moving in the other direction?

Summary

You have learnt to:

- ✓ write user-defined procedures with parameters
- ✓ use the full name of components when referring to them in user-defined procedures
- ✓ use the *Sender* parameter of event-handling procedures
- ✓ use the **Tag** property to pass an integer value to a component, which can be used by the component's event-handlers
- ✓ set several components to use the same event handler

Chapter 18 – Records

Data displayed in a group of text boxes may need to be stored. Single variables could be used, but when they logically belong together, grouping them into records makes the program code more transparent.

Exercise 18.1

- Create the user interface as below:

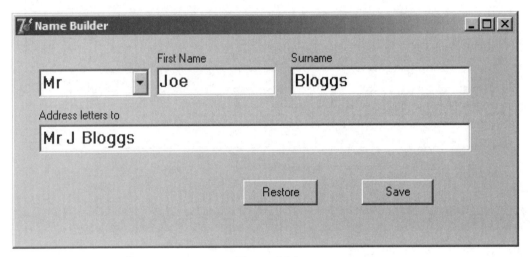

Figure 18.1

The combo box has a set of titles to choose from. The *Address letters to* box content is built up from the title box, the first letter of the first name and the surname. When the *Save* button is pressed, the name elements can be saved in a record variable and the edit boxes cleared. The *Restore* button should refill the edit boxes with the stored name details.

Hints: Use the *LeftStr* function from the **StrUtils** unit to extract the initial letter from the first name. As soon as either title, first name or surname change, the program should adjust A*ddress letters to* name. Use the **OnChange** event to build up the name. Write the code for just one *OnChange* event-handling procedure and then let the other components call that same event (see Exercise 17.1).

Arrays of Records

Usually a set of records is required to be stored. To make these easily accessible, they can be stored in an array.

Exercise 18.2

Adapt the program from Exercise 18.1, so that more than one name can be stored. Add **Previous** and **Next** buttons to allow scrolling through the names. The **New** button clears the text boxes ready for a new entry. Declare an array of records to store the names and use a global variable to point to the current record. Make sure the user cannot go beyond the first and last stored names.

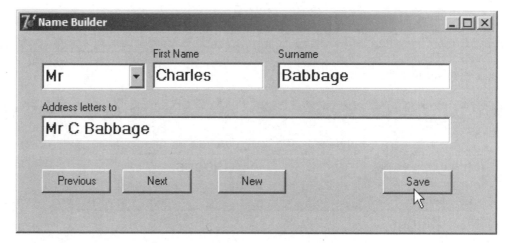

Figure 18.2

Exercise 18.3

Create the following user interface.

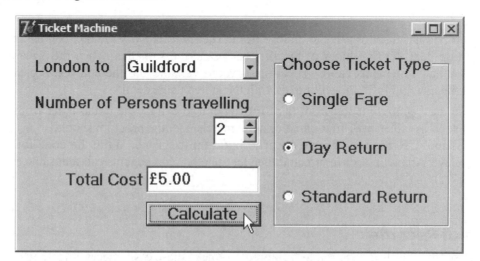

Figure 18.3: Ticket Machine

For each destination in the combobox the different fare costs are stored in a record in an array. The program is to calculate the total cost of tickets from the fare chosen multiplied by the number of persons travelling.

Declare an array of 5 records of the following record type to store details for several destinations.

```
type TDestination = record
    City: String;
    TicketCost: array[0..2] of Currency;
end; {record}
```

Write code to check that destination, ticket type and number of persons have been selected. An item index of −1 for radio groups and comboboxes shows no selection has been made.

In the *FormCreate* event-handler populate the array of records with some test data of your choice.

Exercise 18.4

Adapt the *Format Message* program from Exercise 13.4 to store the selected format together with a user's name, so that a particular user's format preferences can be restored.

Summary

You have learnt to:

- ✓ store data from edit boxes into a record variable
- ✓ store several sets of data from edit boxes in an array of records
- ✓ use an array as a field in a record
- ✓ check that a combo box and a radiogroup have values selected
- ✓ use the following component property

Component	Properties
ComboBox	Text

Chapter 19 – Files

So far, all data was lost when the application terminated. To save data for future use, we can save to computer files. See Chapter 10 for details about types of file.

Writing to a text file

Exercise 19.1

Sending data to a text file allows you to open the file in any text editor to read the content. If you use a filename extension of *.txt*, you can easily open the file using a program such as MS Notepad.

Create a user interface with a list box and a button as shown below:

Form1							
1	33 !	65 A	97 a	129	161 ¡	193 Á	225 á
2	34 "	66 B	98 b	130	162 ¢	194 Â	226 â
3	35 #	67 C	99 c	131	163 £	195 Ã	227 ã
4	36 $	68 D	100 d	132	164 ¤	196 Ä	228 ä
5	37 %	69 E	101 e	133	165 ¥	197 Å	229 å
6	38 &	70 F	102 f	134	166 ¦	198 Æ	230 æ
7	39 '	71 G	103 g	135	167 §	199 Ç	231 ç
8	40 (	72 H	104 h	136	168 ¨	200 È	232 è
9	41)	73 I	105 i	137	169 ©	201 É	233 é
10	42 *	74 J	106 j	138	170 ª	202 Ê	234 ê
11	43 +	75 K	107 k	139	171 «	203 Ë	235 ë
12	44 ,	76 L	108 l	140	172 ¬	204 Ì	236 ì
13	45 -	77 M	109 m	141	173	205 Í	237 í
14	46 .	78 N	110 n	142	174 ®	206 Î	238 î
15	47 /	79 O	111 o	143	175 ¯	207 Ï	239 ï
16	48 0	80 P	112 p	144	176 °	208 Ð	240 ð
17	49 1	81 Q	113 q	145 ´	177 ±	209 Ñ	241 ñ
18	50 2	82 R	114 r	146 ´	178 ²	210 Ò	242 ò
19	51 3	83 S	115 s	147	179 ³	211 Ó	243 ó
20	52 4	84 T	116 t	148	180 ´	212 Ô	244 ô
21	53 5	85 U	117 u	149	181 µ	213 Õ	245 õ
22	54 6	86 V	118 v	150	182 ¶	214 Ö	246 ö
23	55 7	87 W	119 w	151	183 ·	215 ×	247 ÷
24	56 8	88 X	120 x	152	184 ¸	216 Ø	248 ø
25	57 9	89 Y	121 y	153	185 ¹	217 Ù	249 ù
26	58 :	90 Z	122 z	154	186 º	218 Ú	250 ú
27	59 ;	91 [	123 {	155	187 »	219 Û	251 û
28	60 <	92 \	124		156	188 ¼	220 Ü	252 ü
29	61 =	93]	125 }	157	189 ½	221 Ý	253 ý
30	62 >	94 ^	126 ~	158	190 ¾	222 Þ	254 þ
31	63 ?	95 _	127	159	191 ¿	223 ß	255 ÿ
32	64 @	96 `	128 €	160	192 À	224 à	Send to File

Figure 19.1: ASCII codes

In the form's *OnCreate* event-handler write the code to list all the characters represented by the ASCII codes from 1 to 255.

Hint: Use the Chr function to get the character represented by the number supplied as the argument. For example, Chr(65) will return the character 'A'.

For the event-handling procedure for the **Send to File** button you need these statements:

```
var Test : TextFile; // can be declared locally;
begin
  AssignFile(Test, 'Test.txt');
  Rewrite (Test);
    // add statements here to output content of list box
  CloseFile(Test);
end;
```

To output the contents of the list box, you have various options:

```
Writeln (Test, lboCodes.Items.Text);
  // this outputs the contents of the whole list box
```

or

```
for count := 0 to 254
  do
    begin
      Writeln (Test, lboCodes.Items.Strings[Count]);
        // this outputs one line at a time
    end;
```

or

```
Writeln (Test, lboCodes.Items.Strings[lboCodes.ItemIndex]);
    //this outputs the selected item
```

Test your program by checking that the text file lists all the ASCII values and the characters they represent.

Sending output to a printer

As with console applications, to send output to the printer, you write data to a text file, but instead of assigning an external filename to your text file variable, you use `AssignPrn` instead (see Chapter 10).

Exercise 19.2

Adapt your program from Exercise 18.3 by adding a **Buy** button. This button should only be enabled when the user has pressed **Calculate** successfully. Clicking the button should send a ticket to be printed.

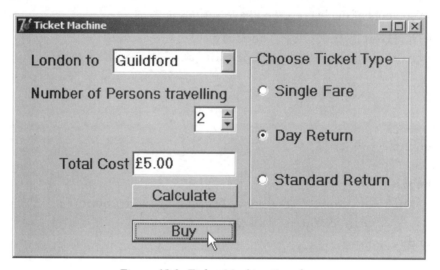

Figure 19.2: Ticket Machine Interface

It should produce output similar to this:

```
*******************************************
*           Day Return Ticket          *
*******************************************
* London to Guildford                  *
*                                      *
* Number of Persons:  2                 *
*                                      *
*  Paid:   £5.00                        *
*******************************************
```

This is an outline of the statement you need:

```
var PrintFile: TextFile;
begin
    AssignPrn (PrintFile);  // assigns the default printer
    Rewrite (PrintFile);
        // Writeln statements to print the ticket go here
    CloseFile (PrintFile)
end;
```

Saving records to a typed file (file of records)

If we want to store data to be read by a program at a later date, it is best to use a file of records for storage. Although these are not text files, you can inspect them in a text editor. Strings will still be recognisable, so it helps when checking whether your program is writing out to the file as expected.

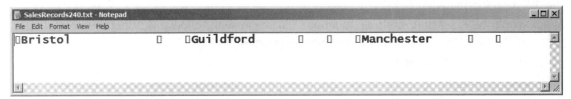

Figure 19.3: File of records opened in a text editor

Exercise 19.3

Extend your program from Exercise 19.2 above, to save data about the ticket sale, so the transport company can calculate takings and other statistics. The program should create a new file for each day of trading.

Open the file in the form's *OnCreate* event-handler, assigning a file name that is unique for every day:

```
AssignFile (SalesFile, 'SalesRecords' +
    IntToStr(DayOfTheYear(Date)) + '.txt');
Rewrite (SalesFile);
```

> This function (from the **DateUtils** unit) supplies the ordinal position of a TDateTime value's day within its year.

Declare a record type with fields *Destination*, *TicketType* and *NoOfPersonsTravelling*.
When a sale is made, the data should be assigned to the record fields and then the record can be saved to the file:

```
Write (SalesFile, SalesRecord);
```

Close the file in *FormClose*:

```
CloseFile (SalesFile);
```

Exercise 19.4

Write a program that reads the file created by your program from Exercise 19.3 and displays the records in a memo box.

Direct Access Files

In a direct access file a record is accessed by calculating an address from its primary key (see Chapter 10).

Exercise 19.5

Adapt your program from Exercise 19.2 to use a direct access file to store the ticket prices for the different destinations.

What would be a sensible hashing function? To begin with, choose destinations that all start with a different letter. Then a simple hashing function might be:

ASCII code of the first letter – 65

First write a program to generate the file of records with destinations and their ticket prices. Then your ticket machine program can read the relevant record to find the ticket prices.

Later you can refine your hashing function to cope with destinations with the same starting letter (by managing synonyms as discussed in Chapter 10).

Exercise 19.6

Adapt your password entry program from Exercise 16.4 to store user IDs and passwords in a direct access file. The user ID can be used as the primary key as it has to be unique. Think of a suitable hashing function, assuming there will not be more than about 20 user IDs stored at any one time.

Summary

You have learnt to:

- ✓ write the contents of a list box to a text file
- ✓ send output to a printer
- ✓ save data records in a typed file
- ✓ use the following component property

Component	Properties
ListBox	Items.Strings[index]

Chapter 20 – Multiple Forms

A Delphi project can consist of more than one form. Most real-world applications consist of more than one form, with one form being the *active* form and the others either *not visible* or *inactive*. A visible form can be made active by clicking on it. If a *modal* form, such as a message box, is visible it is also the active form, and it must be closed before another form can become the active form.

When a new form is created an associated new unit (*.pas* file) is created automatically.

We can also add to a project forms previously created in another project.

Exercise 20.1

This program is going to demonstrate how two forms can use data from each other.

Create a new project and set up the form as Figure 20.1:

Figure 20.1

Then choose **File, New, Form** and set up the components as in Figure 20.2:

Figure 20.2

Write the code for each of the forms:

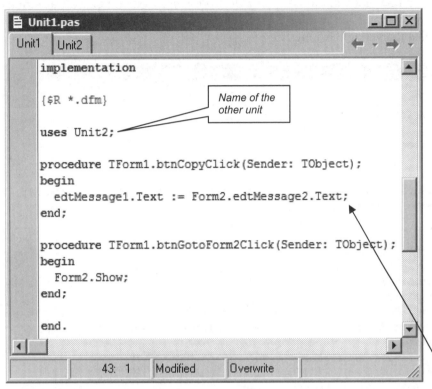

Figure 20.3

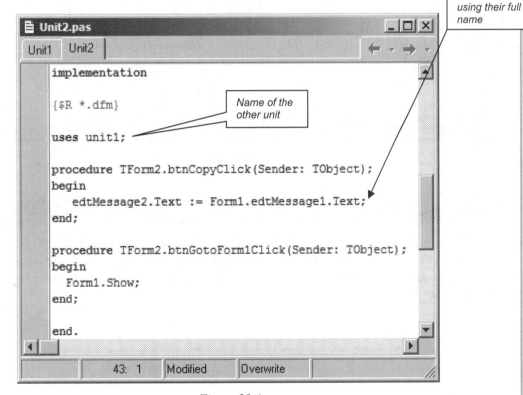

Figure 20.4

Sometimes we may not want to copy a value from a component but we want to make use of a value held in a variable in the other unit. Such a variable needs to be declared in the **public** part of the unit that the variable belongs to:

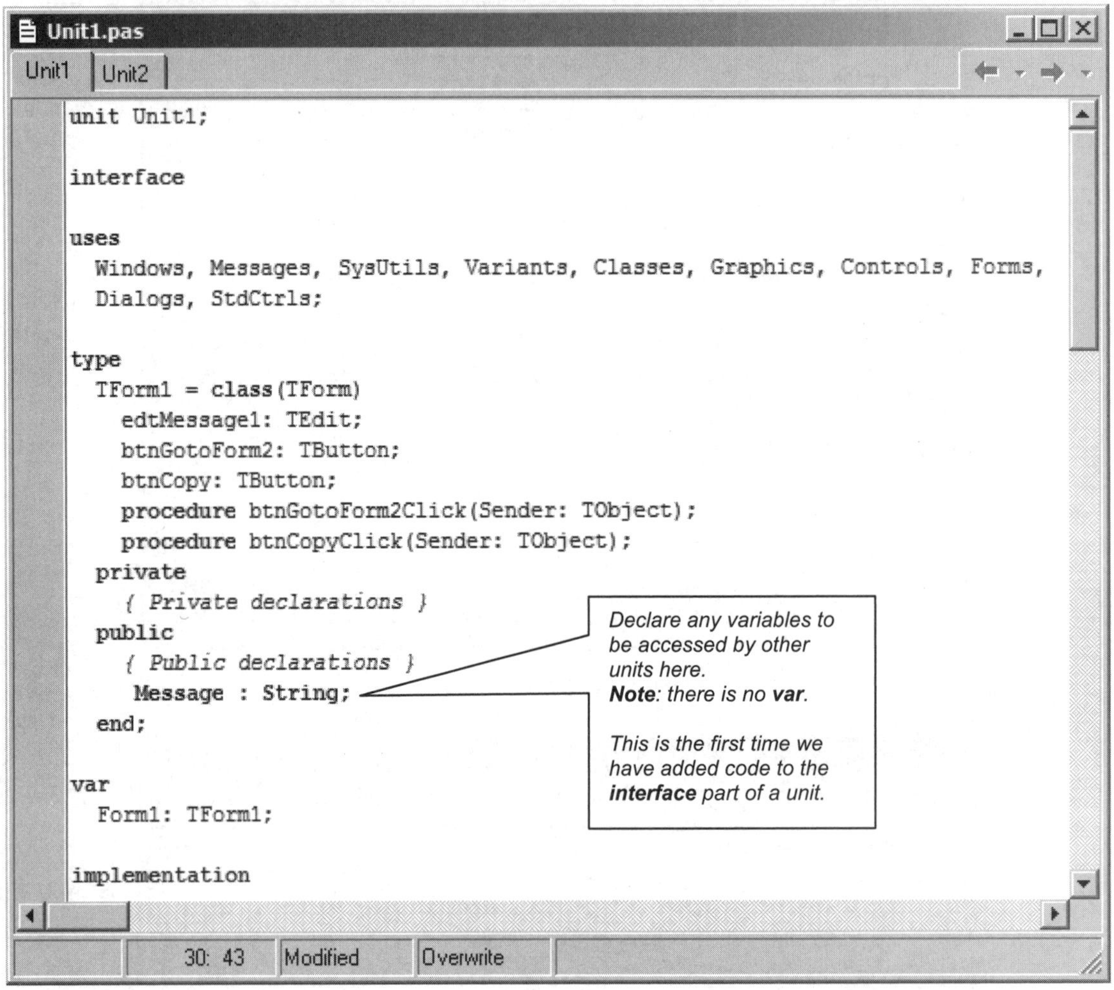

```
Unit1.pas                                                    _ □ ×
Unit1  Unit2                                             ← ▾  → ▾

    unit Unit1;

    interface

    uses
      Windows, Messages, SysUtils, Variants, Classes, Graphics, Controls, Forms,
      Dialogs, StdCtrls;

    type
      TForm1 = class(TForm)
        edtMessage1: TEdit;
        btnGotoForm2: TButton;
        btnCopy: TButton;
        procedure btnGotoForm2Click(Sender: TObject);
        procedure btnCopyClick(Sender: TObject);
      private
        { Private declarations }
      public
        { Public declarations }
        Message : String;
      end;

    var
      Form1: TForm1;

    implementation

    30: 43    Modified    Overwrite
```

Declare any variables to be accessed by other units here.
Note: there is no **var**.

This is the first time we have added code to the **interface** part of a unit.

Figure 20.5

Exercise 20.2

Amend your program from Exercise 20.1, so that the *OnChange* event-handler for **edtMessage1** on *Form1* assigns the edit box's text value to a public variable *Message*. *Form2* reads the public variable and displays its value in the edit box. Note that *Form2* needs to refer to the public variable by its full name: *Form1.Message*.

The following methods can be used to make a form visible:

`Form2.Show`	makes this the active form
`Form2.ShowModal`	makes this the active form, Form1 disabled until Form2 is closed
`Form2.Visible := True`	Form2 becomes the active form only if it was not visible before

Forms are closed with the `Close` statement.

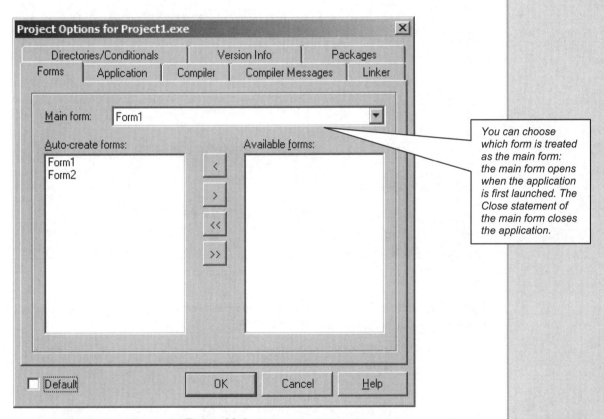

You can choose which form is treated as the main form: the main form opens when the application is first launched. The Close statement of the main form closes the application.

Figure 20.6

It is not very transparent to use form names such as *Form1*. When you want to reuse a form from another project, make sure you save the unit of that form with a unique name. Then you can use it in a new project.

Exercise 20.3

To use the password entry form from Exercise 19.6, make a copy of the folder containing that project. Open the project and use **File, Save As** and type the name *PasswordForm* to duplicate the *.pas* and *.dfm* files. Note that the unit name has now changed:

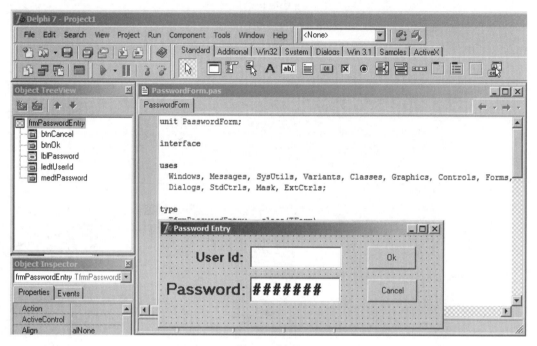

Figure 20.7

If you check the folder where you saved the password entry program, you will see that the unit files are now duplicated, under the new name.

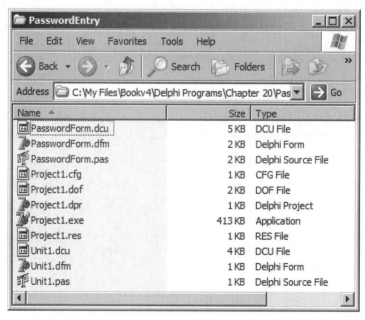

Figure 20.8

- Delete all files except the three *PasswordForm* files.
- Now start a new project and save it to this same folder.
- Select **Project, Add to Project …** and choose *PasswordForm.pas*. Note that you can now choose to view the password entry form with **View, Forms…**.
- On the main form add a button to open the password entry form as a *modal form*, add the **uses** clause and the statement for the button's *OnClick* event-handler:

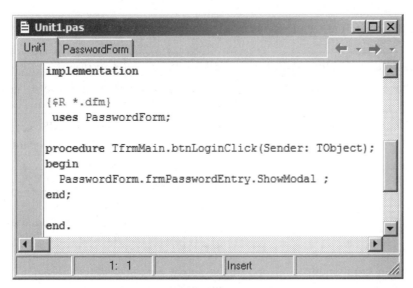

Figure 20.9

Summary

You have learnt to:

- ✓ create a second form.
- ✓ open the second form from the first form and vice versa
    - using `Form.Show`
    - or `Form.ShowModal`
    - or `Form.Visible := True`
- ✓ copy a value from a component in one form to another form using the component's full name.
- ✓ use a value from a public variable in one form in another form using the variable's full name.
- ✓ choose which form is treated as the main form in **Project Options**
- ✓ add a form from another project to a new project, taking care to save units with unique names
- ✓ use the following component property and methods

Component	Properties	Methods
Form	Visible	Show
		ShowModal

Chapter 21 – Databases

Instead of storing data to typed files you can use the table(s) in a database as a data store and display records in Delphi forms.

Delphi has several different technologies available to support database access:

Name of Technology	Abbreviation	Availability	Comment
Borland Database Engine	BDE	Early versions of Delphi	Borland stopped developing this
MS ActiveX Data Objects	ADO	Delphi 5 onwards	Good for MS Access databases on *Windows* operating systems only
InterBase	IBX	Delphi 5 onwards	
dbExpress		Delphi 6 onwards	Recommended by Borland for SQL server database access in Delphi

Besides a **DataSet** component from one of the above data access technologies, you also need the **DataSource** component. This acts as a connector between data-aware controls and a dataset component. Delphi provides **data-aware controls** (in the *Data Controls* page) to view and edit data in a form and these are extensions of standard components such as edit and list boxes, radio buttons, images and grids.

The following exercises use the ADO table and query but other table and query components work in a similar way.

Worked Example A

Using ADO, we can use the **ADOTable** component from the *ADO* components page as our dataset component.

The **DataSource** component is found on the *Data Access* components page.

There are many data-aware components on the *Data Controls* components page. We are going to choose the **DBGrid** so we can display the contents of a whole table from our database.

Before we can make use of a database we need to set one up in *MS Access*.

- Create a folder for this example program. Create a database as *Stock* into this folder.

- Set up a table *Item* in MS Access with the following fields: *ItemCode* (Text), *Description* (Text), *UnitPrice* (Currency), *QuantityInStock* (Number). Add some data of your choice into the table. Do not set a primary key.

- Start a new project and place an **ADOTable**, **DataSource** and **DBGrid** component on a form:

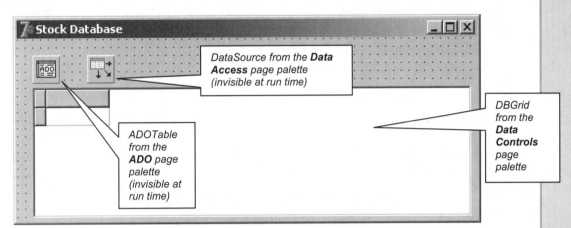

Figure 21.1: Database connection components

- Set the component properties as shown in the table:

Control	Property	Setting
Form1	Name	frmStock
	Caption	Stock Database
ADOTable1	Name	adotItem
		• Click on the ellipsis (**…**) • Click on **Build** in the *ConnectionString* window. This opens another window: *Figure 21.2* • Choose the provider as above.

		• Click on **Next**. • Click on the ellipsis (**…**) • In the next window navigate to the *Stock* database and click on **Open**. • Click on **Test Connection** to check you have successfully connected to your database. • Click **OK** twice to close all *ConnectionString* windows.
	TaleName	Item (from the drop-down list)
	Active	True
DataSource1	Name	dsItem
	DataSet	adotItem (from the drop-down list)
DBGrid1	Name	dbgrdItem
	DataSource	dsItem (from the drop-down list)

- Run the program. You should see the contents of your table displayed in the data grid.
- To adjust the column headings and column widths, click on the … of the *dbgrdItem*'s **Columns** property. This opens this window:

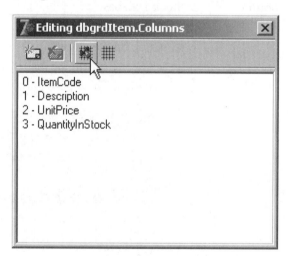

Figure 21.3: The Columns window

- Click on the **Display all fields** icon as above.
- Select each column heading in turn and you will see subproperties. Adjust **Width** and **Alignment**. Then click on the + next to Title. This will give you further subproperties and you can adjust the **Caption** (the text in the column heading).

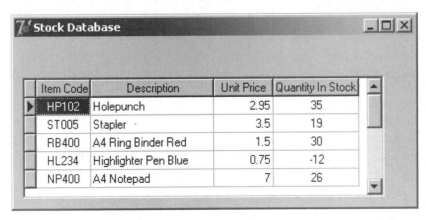

Figure 21.4

- You can edit the fields in the data grid. These changes are saved in the underlying database table. Check it for yourself.

- To navigate through your records easily, add a **DBNavigator** component from the *Data Controls* page to your form. Set its **DataSource** property to *dsItem* (from the drop-down list).

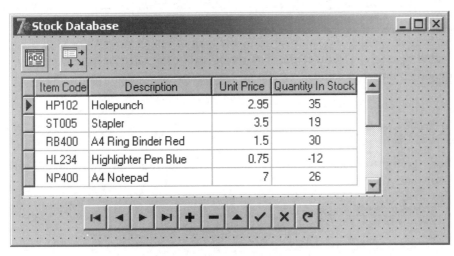

Figure 21.5: The navigator component

- Test that you can navigate through your record set, edit, save, and cancel edits to the current record.

Exercise 21.1

Create your own navigation buttons using the methods in the following table.

First	Calls the dataset's *First* method to set the current record to the first record.
Prior	Calls the dataset's *Prior* method to set the current record to the previous record.
Next	Calls the dataset's *Next* method to set the current record to the next record.
Last	Calls the dataset's *Last* method to set the current record to the last record.
Insert	Calls the dataset's *Insert* method to insert a new record before the current record, and set the dataset to the *Insert* state.
Delete	Deletes the current record. If the **ConfirmDelete** property is True it prompts for confirmation before deleting.
Edit	Puts the dataset in the *Edit* state so that the current record can be modified.
Post	Writes changes in the current record to the database.
Cancel	Cancels edits to the current record, and returns the dataset to *Browse* state.
Refresh	Clears data control display buffers, and then refreshes its buffers from the physical table or query. Useful if the underlying data may have been changed by another application.

Worked Example B

We are now going to add a Search facility. Add a labelled edit box, name it **ledtItemCode**, and a button:

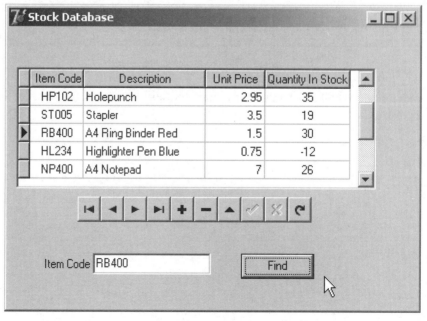

Figure 21.6

To make a record the current record, given its *ItemCode*, we can use the following statement:

```
adotItem.Locate('ItemCode', ledtItemCode.Text,[])
```

- Test your **Find** button.

> **Note:** If the item code does not exist, the current record indicator remains at the previous current record.

Next, we are going to display some of the current record's fields in data-aware edit boxes. The user can type a quantity to order into an edit box and the total cost is going to be displayed in another edit box. When the user clicks on the **Buy** button, the program will automatically reduce the number in stock in the database.

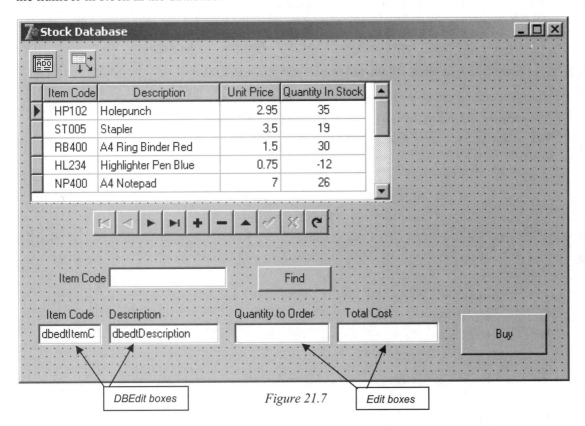

Figure 21.7

- Add the above components to your user interface.

- Set the **Item Code** and **Description** boxes to *ReadOnly*, and their **DataSource** property to *dsItem* (from the drop-down list). Set their **DataField** property to the appropriate field from the drop-down box. This should now display the details of the current record.

The total cost can be calculated from the number entered in the **Quantity to order** box and the *UnitPrice* of the current record.

- Double-click on the **Quantity to Order** edit box and complete the event-handler:

```
procedure TfrmStock.edtQuantityChange(Sender: TObject);
var Quantity : Integer; UnitPrice, Cost : Currency;
begin
  Quantity := StrToInt (edtQuantity.Text);
  UnitPrice := adotItem ['UnitPrice'];
  Cost := Quantity * UnitPrice;
  edtCost.Text := FloatToStrF (Cost, ffCurrency, 5, 2);
end;
```

> *To access a field from a table, give the table name followed by the field name in [ ]*

What happens if you clear the **Quantity to Order** edit box? The *StrToInt* function is not defined when the edit box is empty (or contains a non-number). The debugger message is not very user-friendly. You can trap these foreseeable errors and give the user a more informative message.

- Turn off the debugger: **Select Tools, Debugger Options … , General**.

- Uncheck the **Integrated Debugger** option and click on **OK**.

- Double-click on the **Quantity** edit box and insert the lines as shown:

```
procedure TfrmStock.edtQuantityChange(Sender: TObject);
var Quantity : Integer; UnitPrice, Cost : Currency;
begin
  try
    Quantity := StrToInt (edtQuantity.Text);
    UnitPrice := adotItem ['UnitPrice'];
    Cost := Quantity * UnitPrice;
    edtCost.Text := FloatToStrF(Cost, ffCurrency, 5, 2);
  except
    ShowMessage ('Please enter a number')
  end; {of except}
end;
```

> *Insert the keyword **try** before the statement that might cause a run-time error*

> *And insert the keyword **except** followed by the statements to be obeyed if the above cause a run-time error.*

> *try… **except** clause must finish with **end***

- Now double-click on the **Buy** button and complete the event-handler:

```
procedure TfrmStock.btnBuyClick(Sender: TObject);
var QuantityInStock, QuantityOrdered : Integer;
begin
  QuantityInStock := adotItem['QuantityInStock'];
  QuantityOrdered := StrToInt (edtQuantity.Text);
  QuantityInStock := QuantityInStock - QuantityOrdered;
  adotItem.Edit;   // put data set into edit mode
  adotItem['QuantityInStock'] := QuantityInStock;
  adotItem.Post;  // save the changes
end;
```

Note: If the *Post* method is omitted, the quantity will be reduced in the table but the changes are not saved, and the table will revert to its previous values.

The *Locate* method is fine if we want to just find one record. However, we may want so search for a subset of records from a table and for this we need to use a query.

- Place an **ADOQuery** component from the *ADO* page palette onto your form, with a **DataSource** and **DBGrid**.

- Set the **ConnectionString** as for the ADO table.

- Link the **DataSource** and **DBGrid** to this query component (look for its name in the drop-down boxes).

- Click on the ellipsis (**...**) of the *ADOQuery's* **SQL** property and complete as in Figure 21.8:

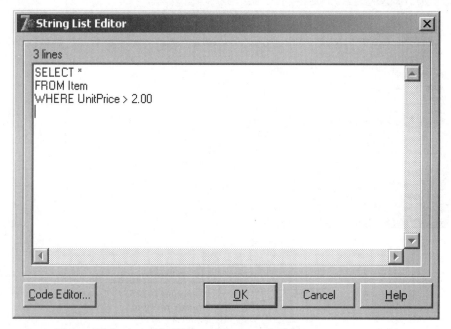

Figure 21.8: A simple SQL statement to find items costing over £2

To run this query, it must be activated.

- Place a button on your form and write the following code in its event-handler:

```
ADOQuery1.Close; //closes the query
ADOQuery1.Open;  // activates the query
```

- Test your query.

Exercise 21.2

Extend the project from the worked example above by allowing customers to place orders. When a new order is placed, the customer name is entered into an edit box. Today's date is automatically entered and an order number generated. When the **Buy** button is clicked, this appends a record into an *OrderLine* table. Add two more tables to your MS Access database:

> Orders (*OrderNo, Date, CustomerName, TotalCost*)
>
> OrderLine (*OrderNo, ItemCode, Quantity, Cost*)

- Extend your user interface as in Figure 21.9:

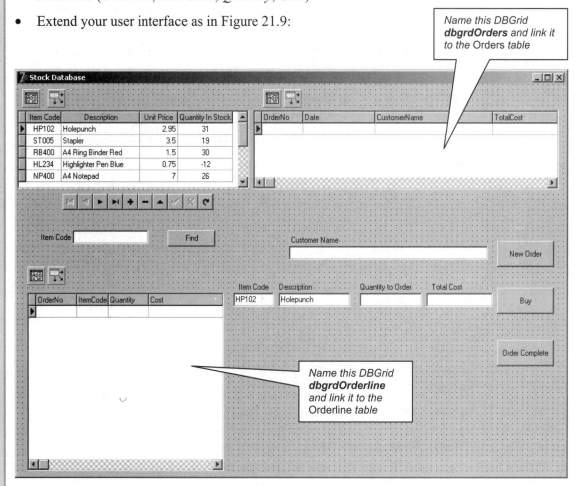

Figure 21.9

- Write the code for the **New Order** button's event-handler. To add a new record, use the *Append* method then assign each field a value. The *TotalCost* field will be updated later. Remember to use the *Post* method to save the record.

Hint: Use the *Order* table's **Tag** property to store the current order number and increment order numbers as new orders are generated. When the form is first created, the tag needs to be updated to the last order number saved in the *Orders* table. Access it with the *Last* method of the *Orders* table.

- Add the necessary code to the **Buy** button, so that a record is added to the *OrderLine* table for each item ordered. Remember to also store the current order number with each item.

Worked Example C

In order to calculate the total cost of one order we need to be able to look at a subset of records in the *OrderLine* table: all those with the current order number. For this we need a parameter query where we can supply the order number at run-time. You can use the ADO query from the worked example. (Rename it *adoqCurrentOrder*.) Check that the connection string is still set correctly and change the **SQL** property as in Figure 21.10:

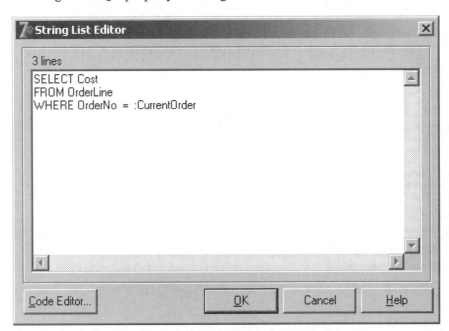

Figure 21.10: SQL statement with parameter

:CurrentOrder is the parameter and we can supply its value at run-time.

- Complete the **Complete Order** button's event-handler as below:

```
procedure TfrmStock.btnOrderCompleteClick(Sender: TObject);
begin
  adoqCurrentOrder.Close;
  adoqCurrentOrder.Parameters[0].Value := adotOrders.Tag;
  adoqCurrentOrder.Open;
end;
```

> This statement supplies a value to the parameter. If there is more than one parameter, the index shows which parameter gets which value.

adoqCurrentOrder will return the dataset where the order number is equal to the last order number. To add all these records' costs together, we need to access each one in turn and add the cost to *Total*.

137

- Add the following statements to the end of the **Complete Order** button's event-handler:

```
Total := 0;
  while not adoqCurrentOrder.Eof
    do
      begin
        Total := Total + adoqCurrentOrder['Cost'];
        adoqCurrentOrder.Next; // move to next record
      end;
```

- Now add the statements to store *Total* in the *TotalCost* field of the current record in the *Orders* table. If you get the error message *Row cannot be located...* add a statement to locate the record with the current order number in the *Orders* table again.

Exercise 21.3

Add a query to your worked example that will find a customer's order by entering the customer's name and the date of the order. Note that when you search on more than one field using the *Locate* method, you need to pass a variant array with the list of values, one for each field. Use the following syntax:

Table1.Locate(*'FieldName1*,…,*FieldNameN'*, VarArrayOf([*'Value1'*,*'Value2'*,….,*'ValueN'*]),[])

Exercise 21.4

Write a simple book loan system. Create tables *Book*, *Borrower* and *Loan*. A borrower is allowed to borrow several books. The program should add a record to the loans table when a borrower takes out a book. Provide the facility to search for a borrower's outstanding books and display them in a data grid.

Summary

You have learnt to:

- ✓ connect an **ADOTable** component to an MS Access database using the **ConnectionString** property
- ✓ connect a **DataSource** to a table component using its **DataSet** property
- ✓ connect a **DBGrid** to a data source in order to display a recordset
- ✓ connect data-aware edit boxes to a data source to display fields of the current record
- ✓ edit the fields in a data grid
- ✓ use the **DBNavigator** component to navigate, edit, add, and delete records in a dataset
- ✓ access a field in the current record of a dataset using the format

    TableName['*FieldName*']

- ✓ use the `try ... except` construct to trap errors and provide more user-friendly messages
- ✓ write an SQL statement to select a subset of a dataset in the format

    ```
    SELECT FieldNames
    FROM DataSetName
    WHERE criteria
    ```

- ✓ activate a query using the *Close* and *Open* methods
- ✓ write an SQL statement that makes use of a parameter
- ✓ supply the parameter at run-time
- ✓ use the following components, properties and methods

Component	Properties	Methods
ADOTable	Name, ConnectionString, TableName, Active	Locate, First, Prior, Next, Last, Insert, Delete, Edit, Post, Cancel, Refresh, Append
DataSource	Name, DataSet	
DBGrid	Name, DataSource, Columns Sub-properties: Width, Alignment, Title, Caption	
DBNavigator	Name, DataSource	
DBEdit	Name, ReadOnly, DataField, DataSource	
ADOQuery	Name, ConnectionString, SQL, Eof	Close, Open

Chapter 22 – Consolidation

Set up an interface with the following components:

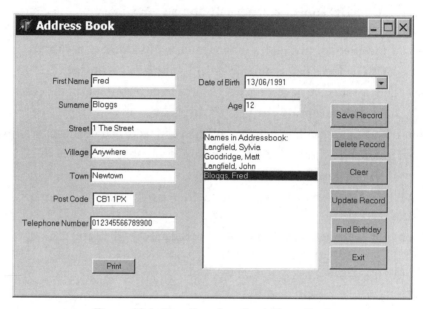

Figure 22.1: User Interface for Address Book

Specification of functionality:

- You need to set up a record structure to save the above personal details. The age should not be saved but calculated for display only.

- The list box should display the full name of all persons held in the address book and when an entry is selected, that person's details should be displayed.

- The current record should be editable, and saved by clicking on the **Update** button.

- The current record should be deleted if the user clicks on the **Delete** button.

- If the user clicks on the **Clear** button, the fields should be cleared, allowing a new record to be entered. This record will be saved when the user clicks on the **Save** button.

- All the details should be saved in a file so they can be accessed at a subsequent running of the program. You may keep all records in an array and write this out to file before exiting the program and read the records from the file into the array when starting the program. You may wish to use an alternative method.

- Clicking on the **Print** button should cause the whole address book to be printed in an 'easy to read' format

- Clicking on the **Find Birthday** button should display a list in a separate window or message box of all birthdays this month.

- Buttons should be enabled or disabled depending on what a user should be allowed to do:

    o When clicking on **Clear**, no Update or Delete should be possible

    o When a person's details are selected no Save should be possible

Part 3

The AQA CPT3 Practical Exercise

In this section:

Chapter 23 –The 2003 Practical Exercise Specification

UKAB Re-marks

Background

The (imaginary) United Kingdom Awarding Body (UKAB) has asked you to design a system for the monitoring of its post-examination re-marks.

If a centre feels that the grade awarded to a candidate for an examination is much lower than expected, the centre can ask for that script to be re-marked. The UKAB expects all re-marks to be completed within three weeks.

The system described in the following specification has been considerably simplified. For example, few subject examinations consist of only one paper. In reality, many details are stored for the purpose of analysis and monitoring.

Specification

1. For any script for which a re-mark is requested, the following details to be stored.

   - Candidate name
   - Candidate number
   - Centre number
   - Subject Reference Code
   - Original mark
   - Re-mark mark (whether changed or unchanged)
   - Whether the centre requested the return of the script.

   You will find it necessary to store other details.

2. For a subject, the following details to be stored.
   - Subject Reference Code
   - Grade boundaries for grades A-E and U

   For the purpose of this exercise, only the following subjects need to be considered.

Subject Reference Code	Grade Boundaries (%)				
	A	B	C	D	E
01325	75	67	60	54	48
20094	70	60	50	40	30
28181	90	78	66	54	42
54821	85	79	74	64	55
64773	68	60	52	46	40

3. The solution must be able to produce a hard copy of the following:
   - a daily list of any re-marks completed where a mark change has affected the grade;
   - a daily list of any re-marks still outstanding, i.e. that have not been completed within a three-week period;
   - a list of re-marks that have been requested for a particular subject;
   - a list of re-marks that have been requested from a particular centre.

4. The solution must produce a document to be returned to the centre giving the results of the re-mark. This document should display the UKAB logo. The following details should be included in this document.
   - Centre number
   - Candidate name
   - Candidate number
   - Subject Reference Code
   - Original mark
   - Original grade
   - Either the re-mark mark and grade, if changed, or a sentence to say that there has been no change.

5. Test data for at least 15 candidates from 4 centres and the subjects listed above should cover situations in which marks are both increased and decreased.

6. (i) Candidate numbers are of 4 digits and will be unique within any centre, but not between centres. The solution should ensure that this is allowed for.
   (ii) Centre numbers are allocated within the range 10000 to 80000 and are unique.
   (iii) Subject Reference Codes are 5 numeric digits.

Requirements of the Practical Exercise

Candidates are expected to design and implement an appropriate computing system and provide sufficient documentation to demonstrate the following practical skills:
- Design
- Implement / Test

The task may be undertaken by:

either writing a program in a chosen high level language

or using a suitable application package.

Candidates are expected to produce brief documentation including some of all of the following, as appropriate.

Design

- Definition of data requirements
- User interface design including output, forms and reports
- Method of data entry, including validation
- Record structure, file organisation and processing
- Security and integrity of data
- System design

Implementation / Testing

- Hard copy output to prove the correct working of the system
- Hard copy of solution, e.g. annotated program listing, spreadsheet showing formulae, appropriate listings from a database

This documentation is to be brought to the examination and handed in with the candidate's answer script for Unit 3 (CPT3) at the end of the examination. A Cover Sheet, signed by the teacher and the candidate, authenticating the work of the candidate, must be attached to the documentation.

Chapter 24 – Solution using Pascal

The following pages contain the documentation for a model answer for the 2003 Practical Exercise. On pages *P-45* to *P-48* are selected questions from the AQA May 2003 question paper with answers, including the reference to evidence from the following documentation.

Analysis

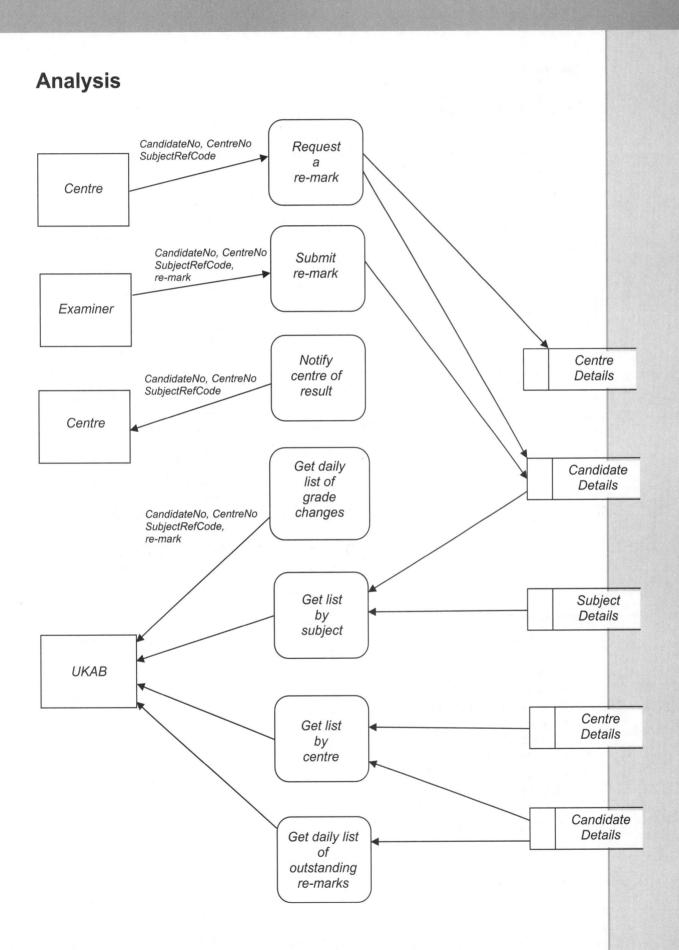

Design

Data Requirements

Required by specification	Required on document to centre	Extra fields	Field Name	Notes
Y	Y		CentreNumber	Unique when combined (Centre could ask for re-mark of several subjects for same candidate)
Y	Y		CandidateNumber	
Y	Y		SubjectRefCode	
Y	Y		CandidateName	
		Y	CentreAddress	So document can be sent to centre
	Y		OrigGrade	Could be **calculated** from subject details
	Y		ReMarkGrade	Could be **calculated** from subject details
Y	Y		OrigMark	whole number between 1 and 100
Y	Y		ReMark	whole number between 1 and 100
Y			GradeBoundary	Need this for A, B, C, D, E (whole number between 1 and 100)
Y			ScriptReturn	Boolean, whether centre requested return of script
		Y	DateRemark	Needed to determine daily list
		Y	DateRequest	Needed to determine outstanding re-marks

Menu Design

1 – New Request
2 – Delete Request
3 – Enter Re-mark
4 – Daily List of Grade Changes
5 – Daily List of Outstanding Re-marks
6 – Subject List
7 – Centre List
8 – Letter to Centre
9 – List records
10 – Exit Program

Enter option number: --

Printed Output Design

```
Requests by Subject Ref Code xxxxx  xx/xx/xxxxx
=================================================

Date         Centre  Candidate Original Original Remark New
Requested    Number  Number    Mark     Grade    Mark   Grade
xx/xx/xxxx   xxxxx   xxxx      xx       X        xx     X
```

```
Today's Remarks resulting in Grade Changes  xx/xx/xxxxx
=======================================================

Date         Centre  Candidate Subject  Orig. Orig. Remark New
Requested    Number  Number    Ref Code Mark  Grade Mark   Grade
xx/xx/xxxx   xxxxx   xxxx      xxxxx    xx    X     xx     X
```

```
Requests by Centre xxxx  xx/xx/xxxxx
====================================

Date         Candidate Subject  Original Original Remark New
Requested    Number    Ref Code Mark     Grade    Mark   Grade
xx/xx/xxxx   xxxxx     xxxxx    xx       X        xx     X
```

Chosen Font: Courier New Size: 14

Letter to Centre (leave enough space for letterhead, 15 lines):

Chosen Font:
Courier New
Size: 14

```
Centre Number : xxxxx
Centre Address : xxxxxxxxxxxxxxxxxxxxxxxxxxxxxxxxxx
                                        xx/xx/xxxx
Result of remark request
========================

Candidate Candidate              Subject  Original Original
Number    Name                   Ref Code Mark     Grade
xxxx      xxxxxxxxxxxxxxxxxxxxxxx xxxxx    xx       X


No changes to marks or grade

Or

The revised number of marks is  xx.
No change of grade.

Or

The revised number of marks is  xx.
Revised grade:  X.
```

Record Structure and File Organisation

Subject File (Direct Access)

Hashing Algorithm: use last 2 digits as address (No collisions with given subject codes)

Field Name	Data Type	Length	Validation	Comment
SubjectRefCode	String	5	5 digits, must exist	Unique (key)
Boundary	Array ['A'..'E'] of Integer			Stores boundary mark for respective grades

Centre File (Serial Access)

Field Name	Data Type	Length	Validation	Comment
CentreNumber	Integer		Between 10000 and 80000	Unique (key)
CentreAddress	String	150		Includes Centre Name

Candidate File (Serial Access)

Field Name	Data Type	Length	Validation	Comment
CentreNumber	Integer		Must exist in Centre File	Composite key (CandidateNumber unique to Centre)
CandidateNumber	String	4	4 digits	
CandidateName	String	25		

Request File (Serial File)

Field Name	Data Type	Length	Validation	Comment
CentreNumber	Integer		Must exist in Candidate File	Unique (Composite key)
CandidateNumber	String	4		
SubjectRefCode	String	5	Must exist in Subject file	
OrigMark	Byte		Between 0 and 100	
ReMark	Byte		Between 0 and 100	
OrigGrade	Character	1	Looked up from Subject file	
ReGrade	Character	1	Looked up from Subject file	
ScriptReturn	Boolean			Only one of two possible values
DateRequest	Date		System date	Today's date when request is entered into system
DateRemark	Date		System date	Today's date when remark is entered into system

Testplan

make up 15 candidates
make up 4 centres
make up requests (about 20 requests)

must have the following cases:

remarks more than original mark
remark less than original mark

no change in grade
change in grade

1 or more requests from a centre
0, 1 or more requests per subject

requests outstanding after 3 weeks

extra:
candidates with remarks for several subjects

Test Number	Test Type	Evidence Page Number
1	Main Menu	11
2	Validation of centre number	11
3	Validation of candidate number	11
4	Validation of subject reference code	12
5	Validation of marks	12
6	correct grade is looked up	12,14
6,7,8	records are stored and retrieved correctly	12,13,14
9	Unique requests	14
10	list of requests by subject reference code	15
11	list of requests by centre	16
12	Daily list of grade changes	17
13	Daily list of outstanding re-marks	18
14	Document to centre with and without mark/grade change	19-21

Candidate Name	Centre Number	Cand. Number	Subject Ref Code	Orig. Marks	Grade*	re-mark Marks	Grade*	grade change*	Script return ?	Date remark was requested*	Date script was remarked*	Reason for choice
Mickey Mouse	12345	2345	54821	45	U	55	E	Y	Y	26-Mar-03	27-Mar-03	E borderline after re-mark
Jimmy Nail	12345	4556	54821	84	B	85	A	Y	Y	26-Mar-03	31-Mar-03	more than one candidate from this centre
Jack Sprat	12345	7799	01325	47	U	51	E		Y	26-Mar-03	31-Mar-03	1 mark off an E before re-mark
Oliver Twist	22151	1001	54821	70	D	73	D		Y	26-Mar-03	31-Mar-03	1 mark off a C after re-mark
Joe Bloggs	22151	1234	01325	58	D	55	D			26-Mar-03	31-Mar-03	
Joe Bloggs	22151	1234	20094	35	E	32	E			26-Mar-03	31-Mar-03	more than one subject from this candidate
Joe Bloggs	22151	1234	28181	40	U				Y	26-Mar-03		overdue
Joe Bloggs	22151	1234	54821	50	U	49	U			26-Mar-03	31-Mar-03	
Chris Evans	22151	4455	54821	76	C	80	B	Y		26-Mar-03	31-Mar-03	grade change up
Tom Thumb	22151	4567	01325	66	C	59	D	Y	Y	26-Mar-03	31-Mar-03	grade change down
Jemima Spratt	22151	5678	01325	99	A	100	A			26-Mar-03	31-Mar-03	extreme marks
Anna Karenina	22151	6789	01325	0	U	0	U			26-Mar-03	31-Mar-03	extreme marks
Anna Karenina	22151	6789	54821	63	E				Y	26-Mar-03		overdue
Violet Day	22151	7456	54821	72	D					26-Mar-03		overdue
Fred Flintstone	23456	2222	54821	84	B	85	A	Y	Y	26-Mar-03	31-Mar-03	1 centre 1 request, borderline A after re-mark
Rose Budd	77777	0100	28181	65	D					26-Mar-03		overdue, leading zero in Cand. No.
Donald Duck	77777	1234	54821	47	U					26-Mar-03		same CandNo as centre 22151
Jack Russell	80000	3456	28181	50	E					26-Mar-03		overdue, centre No extreme
Jack Russell	10000	3456	54821	19	U					26-Mar-03		overdue, centre No. extreme

Candidate Name	Centre Number	Cand. Number	Subject Ref Code	Orig. Marks	Grade*	re-mark Marks	Grade*	grade change*	Script return?	Date remark was requested*	Date script was remarked*	Reason for choice
Jimmy Nail	12345	4556	93421	34					Y	26-Mar-03		wrong subject code, but hashes to a subject record
	80001											invalid centre number
	9999											invalid centre number
	abcde											invalid centre number
	empty string											no centre number entered
		234										invalid candidate number
		34567										invalid candidate number
		abc										invalid candidate number
		empty string										no candidate number
			abcde									invalid subject code
			3421									invalid subject code
			933421									invalid subject code
			empty string									no subject code
				-1								invalid marks
				101								invalid marks
				empty string								no marks
				a								invalid marks

* means data not entered, but calculated by program, just in table for checking

bold are those entries I expect to see in lists by centre (22151), subject ref code (54821), grade changes (25/3/03), subject ref code (54821), grade changes (25/3/03),

Overdue (on and after 10/4/03)

Testing

Test		
| 1<br><br>2 | ```
┌─ C:\My Files\Computing AS\CPT3\confidential\[
│
│
│    UKAB Remark Service
│    ==================
│
│    Please choose an option
│
│    1 - New Request
│    2 - Delete Request
│    3 - Enter Remark
│    4 - Daily List of Grade Changes
│    5 - Daily List of Outstanding Re-Marks
│    6 - Subject List
│    7 - Centre List
│    8 - Letter to Centre
│    9 - List records on screen
│    10 - Exit Program
│
│    Enter Option Number: 1
│ Centre Number: 80001
│ Centre Number must be between 10000 and 80000
│ Centre Number: 9999
│ Centre Number must be between 10000 and 80000
│ Centre Number: abcde
│ Centre Number must be between 10000 and 80000
│ Centre Number:
│ Centre Number must be between 10000 and 80000
│ Centre Number: 12345
│ Centre Address: High School, LowTown
``` | Main Menu<br><br><br><br><br><br>User chose 'New Request'<br><br>testing validation of centre number works (i.e. Must be a number between 10000 and 80000). If centre not previously entered, it asks for a centre address. |
| 3 | ```
┌─ C:\My Files\Computing AS\CPT3\confidential\[
│ Centre Number: 12345
│ Centre Address: High School, LowTown
│ Candidate Number:  234
│ Candidate Number must have 4 digits.
│ Candidate Number:  34567
│ Candidate Number must have 4 digits.
│ Candidate Number:  abcd
│ Candidate Number must have 4 digits.
│ Candidate Number:
│ Candidate Number must have 4 digits.
│ Candidate Number:  2345
│ Candidate Name: Mickey Mouse
``` | This is a continuation of the above. Now testing the validation of Candidate Number. (i.e. must be 4 digits). If candidate not previously entered into system it will ask for a candidate name |

| 4<br><br>5<br><br>6 | ```
█ C:\My Files\Computing AS\CPT3\confidenti
    Enter Option Number: 1
Centre Number: 12345
Centre Address: High School, Low Road, AnyTown
Candidate Number:  2345
Candidate Name: Mickey Mouse
Subject Reference Code: abcde
Subject Ref Code must be 5 digits.
Subject Reference Code: 3421
Subject Ref Code must be 5 digits.
Subject Reference Code: 933421
Subject Ref Code must be 5 digits.
Subject Reference Code: 93421
Subject Ref Code must be 5 digits.
Subject Reference Code: 54821
Original Mark: -1
Marks must be between 0 and 100
Original Mark: 101
Marks must be between 0 and 100
Original Mark:
Marks must be between 0 and 100
Original Mark: a
Marks must be between 0 and 100
Original Mark: 45
Script to be returned? Y/N: Y

Date request received:   26/03/2003
Centre Number:           12345
Candidate Number:        2345
Subject Reference Code: 54821
Original Mark/ Grade:    45  U
Re-mark Mark / Grade:    0
Re-mark received:
Script return:           Yes
Save this record? Y/N
``` | This is testing the validation of the subject reference code. It must have 5 digits. But it also must exist in the subject file. That is why it rejects 93421, even though this number will hash to the same direct access address as an existing subject code.<br><br>This tests that marks entered are between 0 and 100.<br><br>Here a request record is shown, note the correct grade. |
| 7 | ```
█ C:\My Files\Computing AS\CPT3\X06 Implementation\
UKAB Remark Service
===================

Please choose an option

1 - New Request
2 - Delete Request
3 - Enter Remark
4 - Daily List of Grade Changes
5 - Daily List of Outstanding Re-Marks
6 - Subject List
7 - Centre List
8 - Letter to Centre
9 - List records on screen
10 - Exit Program

Enter Option Number: 3
Candidate Number:  2345
Centre Number: 12345
Subject Reference Code: 54821

Date request received:  20/03/2003
Centre Number / Address:12345   Ideal School New Town
Candidate Number:        2345
Candidate Name:          Mickey Mouse
Subject Reference Code: 54821
Original Mark/ Grade:    45  U
Re-mark Mark / Grade:    0
Re-mark received:
Script return:           Yes
Is this the record you wish to update? Y/N Y
Enter new mark: 55
``` | A remark mark is to be entered. It checks with the user that this is the correct request for updating. |

| 8 | ```
┌──────────────────────────────────────────────┐
│ ▣  C:\My Files\Computing AS\CPT3\confidential\│
├──────────────────────────────────────────────┤
      9 - List records on screen
     10 - Exit Program

      Enter Option Number: 9
No of Centres: 6
No of Candidates: 15
No of Requests: 19
12345 High School, Low Road, AnyTown
22151 Long Road College Cambridge
23456 Rock College
77777 High Hill, Anywhere
80000 The Last College, EndOfTheWorld
10000 The First College, BeginningoftheWorld
12345 2345  Mickey Mouse
12345 4556  Jimmy Nail
12345 7799  Jack Sprat
22151 1001  Oliver Twist
22151 1234  Joe Bloggs
22151 4455  Chris Evans
22151 4567  Tom Thumb
22151 5678  Jemima Spratt
22151 6789  Anna Karenina
22151 7456  Violet Day
23456 2222  Fred Flintstone
77777 0100  Rose Budd
77777 1234  Donald Duck
80000 3456  Jack Russell
10000 3456  Jack Russell
``` | This lists all records currently in the system. Note that it also shows overall number of centres, candidates and requests entered. |
| 8 cont. | ```
┌──────────────────────────────────────────────┐
│ ▣  Select C:\My Files\Computing AS\CPT3\confider│
├──────────────────────────────────────────────┤
10000 3456   Jack Russell
 12345 2345 54821 45 U  0     TRUE 26/03/2003
 12345 4556 54821 84 B  0     TRUE 26/03/2003
 12345 7799 01325 47 U  0     TRUE 26/03/2003
 22151 1001 54821 70 D  0     TRUE 26/03/2003
 22151 1234 01325 58 D  0    FALSE 26/03/2003
 22151 1234 20094 35 E  0    FALSE 26/03/2003
 22151 1234 28181 40 U  0     TRUE 26/03/2003
 22151 1234 54821 50 U  0    FALSE 26/03/2003
 22151 4455 54821 76 C  0    FALSE 26/03/2003
 22151 4567 01325 66 C  0     TRUE 26/03/2003
 22151 5678 01325 99 A  0    FALSE 26/03/2003
 22151 6789 01325  0 U  0    FALSE 26/03/2003
 22151 6789 54821 63 E  0     TRUE 26/03/2003
 22151 7456 54821 72 D  0    FALSE 26/03/2003
 23456 2222 54821 84 B  0     TRUE 26/03/2003
 77777 0100 28181 65 D  0    FALSE 26/03/2003
 77777 1234 54821 47 U  0    FALSE 26/03/2003
 80000 3456 28181 50 E  0    FALSE 26/03/2003
 10000 3456 54821 19 U  0    FALSE 26/03/2003  ▮
``` | This is a continuation of the above. |

```
 C:\My Files\Computing AS\CPT3\confidential\
22151 7456 54821 72 D 0    FALSE 26/03/2003
23456 2222 54821 84 B 0     TRUE 26/03/2003
77777 0100 28181 65 D 0    FALSE 26/03/2003
77777 1234 54821 47 U 0    FALSE 26/03/2003
80000 3456 28181 50 E 0    FALSE 26/03/2003
10000 3456 54821 19 U 0    FALSE 26/03/2003



    UKAB Remark Service
    ====================

    Please choose an option

    1 - New Request
    2 - Delete Request
    3 - Enter Remark
    4 - Daily List of Grade Changes
    5 - Daily List of Outstanding Re-Marks
    6 - Subject List
    7 - Centre List
    8 - Letter to Centre
    9 - List records on screen
    10 - Exit Program

    Enter Option Number: 1
Centre Number: 10000
Candidate Number:  3456
Subject Reference Code: 54821
Not a unique request. Please check your details.
```

This tests that the user can't input the same request twice. At the top of this screenshot is still visible part of the list of records currently in the system. The user is trying to enter the last one again.

9

```
 C:\My Files\Computing AS\CPT3\confidential\Delphi Sol
12345 2345 54821 45 U 55 E  TRUE 26/03/2003 27/03/2003
12345 4556 54821 84 B 85 A  TRUE 26/03/2003 31/03/2003
12345 7799 01325 47 U 51 E  TRUE 26/03/2003 31/03/2003
22151 1001 54821 70 D 73 D  TRUE 26/03/2003 31/03/2003
22151 1234 01325 58 D 55 D FALSE 26/03/2003 31/03/2003
22151 1234 20094 35 E 32 E FALSE 26/03/2003 31/03/2003
22151 1234 28181 40 U 0     TRUE 26/03/2003
22151 1234 54821 50 U 49 U FALSE 26/03/2003 31/03/2003
22151 4455 54821 76 C 80 B FALSE 26/03/2003 31/03/2003
22151 4567 01325 66 C 59 D  TRUE 26/03/2003 31/03/2003
22151 5678 01325 99 A100 A FALSE 26/03/2003 31/03/2003
22151 6789 01325  0 U  0 U FALSE 26/03/2003 31/03/2003
22151 6789 54821 63 E 0     TRUE 26/03/2003
22151 7456 54821 72 D 0    FALSE 26/03/2003
23456 2222 54821 84 B 85 A  TRUE 26/03/2003 31/03/2003
77777 0100 28181 65 D 0    FALSE 26/03/2003
77777 1234 54821 47 U 0    FALSE 26/03/2003
80000 3456 28181 50 E 0    FALSE 26/03/2003
10000 3456 54821 19 U 0    FALSE 26/03/2003



    UKAB Remark Service
    ====================

    Please choose an option

    1 - New Request
    2 - Delete Request
    3 - Enter Remark
    4 - Daily List of Grade Changes
    5 - Daily List of Outstanding Re-Marks
    6 - Subject List
    7 - Centre List
```

This shows the records after all the test data has been entered.

```
Requests by Subject Ref Code 54821   31/03/2003

===============================================
```

Date Requested	Centre Number	Candidate Number	Original Mark	Original Grade	Remark Mark	New Grade
26/03/2003	12345	2345	45	U	55	E
26/03/2003	12345	4556	84	B	85	A
26/03/2003	22151	1001	70	D	73	D
26/03/2003	22151	1234	50	U	49	U
26/03/2003	22151	4455	76	C	80	B
26/03/2003	22151	6789	63	E		
26/03/2003	22151	7456	72	D		
26/03/2003	23456	2222	84	B	85	A
26/03/2003	77777	1234	47	U		
26/03/2003	10000	3456	19	U		

Q1(a)(ii)

Note: This is evidence for Q1(a)(ii) and so is labelled as such in the examination

Requests by Centre 22151   31/03/2003

=======================================

Date Requested	Candidate Number	Subject Ref Code	Original Mark	Original Mark	Remark Mark	New Grade
26/03/2003	1001	54821	70	D	73	D
26/03/2003	1234	01325	58	D	55	D
26/03/2003	1234	20094	35	E	32	E
26/03/2003	1234	28181	40	U		
26/03/2003	1234	54821	50	U	49	U
26/03/2003	4455	54821	76	C	80	B
26/03/2003	4567	01325	66	C	59	D
26/03/2003	5678	01325	99	A	100	A
26/03/2003	6789	01325	0	U	0	U
26/03/2003	6789	54821	63	E		
26/03/2003	7456	54821	72	D		

Today's Remarks resulting in Grade Changes 31/03/2003

==

Date Requested	Centre Number	Candidate Number	Subject Ref Code	Orig. Mark	Orig. Grade	Remark Mark	New Grade	
26/03/2003	12345	4556	54821	84	B	85	A	
26/03/2003	12345	7799	01325	47	U	51	E	
26/03/2003	22151	4455	54821	76	C	80	B	
26/03/2003	22151	4567	01325	66	C	59	D	Q 4 (c) (ii)
26/03/2003	23456	2222	54821	84	B	85	A	

Q 2 (a) (ii)

Requests outstanding after 3 weeks as on 01/05/2003

==

Date Requested	Centre Number	Candidate Number	Subject Ref Code	Original Mark	Original Grade
26/03/2003	22151	1234	28181	40	U
26/03/2003	22151	6789	54821	63	E
26/03/2003	22151	7456	54821	72	D
26/03/2003	77777	0100	28181	65	D
26/03/2003	77777	1234	54821	47	U
26/03/2003	80000	3456	28181	50	E
26/03/2003	10000	3456	54821	19	U

United Kingdom Awarding Body

Centre Number : 22151

Centre Address: Long Road College Cambridge

31/03/2003

Result of remark request
========================

Candidate Number	Candidate Name	Subject Ref Code	Original Mark	Original Grade
6789	Anna Karenina	01325	0	U

No change to marks or grade

Q3 (a) (i)

Q3 (b)

United Kingdom Awarding Body

```
Centre Number : 22151
Centre Address: Long Road College Cambridge
                                          31/03/2003
Result of remark request
=========================

Candidate   Candidate              Subject   Original  Original
Number      Name                   Ref Code  Mark      Grade
1001                Oliver Twist   54821     70        D


The revised number of marks is   73.
No change of grade
```

Q 4 (c) (i)

United Kingdom Awarding Body

Centre Number : 22151

Centre Address: Long Road College Cambridge

31/03/2003

Result of remark request

=========================

Candidate Number	Candidate Name	Subject Ref Code	Original Mark	Original Grade
4455	Chris Evans	54821	76	C

The revised number of marks is   80.

Revised grade: B

Note: *This is a blank copy of the letter-headed paper used for the Letter to Centre*

United Kingdom Awarding Body

```
Program UKABinitialiseFiles; {Author Sylvia Langfield}

{$APPTYPE CONSOLE}

Uses
  SysUtils;

Type TCentre = Record
                 CentreNumber : Integer;
                 CentreAddress : String[150];
               End;


Type TCandidate = Record
                    CandidateNumber : String[4];
                    CandidateName : String[25];
                    CentreNumber : Integer;
                  End;


Type TRequest = Record
                  CandidateNumber : String[4];
                  CentreNumber : Integer;
                  SubjectRefCode : String[5];
                  OrigMark : Byte;
                  ReMark : Byte;
                  OrigGrade : Char;
                  ReGrade : Char;
                  ScriptReturn : Boolean;
                  DateRequest : TDateTime;
                  DateRemark : TDateTime;
                End;

Var
  RequestFile : File Of TRequest;
  CandidateFile : File Of TCandidate;
  CentreFile : File Of TCentre;
  Centre : TCentre;
  Candidate : TCandidate;
  Request : TRequest;
```

```
// ************* Main program body ********************************
Begin
      {set up dummy records }
    Centre.CentreNumber := 0;
    Candidate.CentreNumber := 0;
    Request.CentreNumber := 0;

    {set up Requests File}
    AssignFile (RequestFile,'UKABRequests.dat');
    ReWrite (RequestFile);
    Write (RequestFile,Request);
    CloseFile (RequestFile);

    {set up Centre File}
    AssignFile (CentreFile,'UKABCentres.dat');
    ReWrite (CentreFile);
    Write (CentreFile,Centre);
    CloseFile (CentreFile);

    {set up Candidate File}
    AssignFile (CandidateFile,'UKABCandidates.dat');
    ReWrite (CandidateFile);
    Write (CandidateFile,Candidate);
    CloseFile (CandidateFile);
End.
```

```pascal
Program UKABEnterGradeBoundaries;    {Author S Langfield}

{$APPTYPE CONSOLE}

Uses
  SysUtils, StrUtils;


Type TSubject = Record
                  SubjectRefCode : String[5];
                  Boundary : Array ['A'..'E'] Of Integer;
                End;
Var
  Subject :  TSubject;
  SubjectFile : File Of TSubject;
  Grade : Char; Position : Byte; Value, Dummy : Integer;


Function Hash (S : String) : Byte;
{Hashing Algorithm: gets last 2 digits of Subject Ref Code and makes it into a
number}
Var
  V, Dummy : Integer;
  Begin
    S := MidStr(S,4,2);
    Val(S, V, Dummy);
    Hash := V;
  End;
//************** Main Program Body ********************
Begin
  AssignFile (SubjectFile,'UKABSubjects.dat');
  ReWrite (SubjectFile);        //open file for writing
  Write ('Enter subject code: (X to finish) ');
  Readln(Subject.SubjectRefCode);
  While Subject.SubjectRefCode <> 'X'
    Do
      Begin
        For Grade := 'A' To 'E'
          Do
            Begin
              Write('enter ',Grade,' grade boundary: ');
              Readln (Subject.Boundary[Grade]);
            End;
        Position := Hash (Subject.SubjectRefCode);
        Seek (SubjectFile,Position);
        Write(SubjectFile,Subject); //output subject record to file
        Write ('Enter subject code: (X to finish) ');
        Readln(Subject.SubjectRefCode);
      End;
  CloseFile(SubjectFile);
End.
```

```pascal
Program UKABremarkService; {Author: Sylvia Langfield}
{$APPTYPE CONSOLE}
Uses
  SysUtils, StrUtils, Printers, Graphics;

Const
  MaxCentres = 10;
  MaxCandidates = 30;
  MaxRequests = 50;
  RequestFileName = 'UKABRequests.dat';
  CentreFileName =  'UKABCentres.dat';
  CandidateFileName = 'UKABCandidates.dat';

Type TSubject = Record
                SubjectRefCode : String[5];
                Boundary : Array ['A'..'E'] Of Integer;
              End;

Type TCentre = Record    {Store no. of centres in 1st record}
                CentreNumber : Integer;
                CentreAddress : String[150];
              End;

Type TCandidate = Record {Store no. of candidates in 1st record}
                CandidateNumber : String[4];
                CandidateName : String[25];
                CentreNumber : Integer;
              End;

Type TRequest = Record {Store no. of requests in 1st record}
                CandidateNumber : String[4];
                CentreNumber : Integer;
                SubjectRefCode : String[5];
                OrigMark : Byte;
                ReMark : Byte;
                OrigGrade : Char;
                ReGrade : Char;
                ScriptReturn : Boolean;
                DateRequest : TDateTime;      Q1 (a) (i)
                DateRemark : TDateTime;
              End;
```

```
Var
  Subject : TSubject;
  Centre : Array [1..MaxCentres] Of TCentre;
  Candidate : Array [1..MaxCandidates] Of TCandidate;
  Request : Array [1..MaxRequests] Of TRequest;


  SubjectFile : File Of TSubject;
  CentreFile : File Of TCentre;
  CandidateFile : File Of TCandidate;
  RequestFile : File Of TRequest;

  NoOfRequests : Integer;
  NoOfCentres : Integer;
  NoOfCandidates : Integer;
  Finished : Boolean;

  Output : TextFile;

{*********** File Load & save Routines ***********************}

Procedure LoadFiles;
Var
  Count : Integer;
  DummyRequest : TRequest;
  DummyCentre: TCentre;
  DummyCandidate : TCandidate;
  Begin
    {Load centre file}
    AssignFile (CentreFile, CentreFileName);
    Reset (CentreFile);
    Read (CentreFile, DummyCentre);
    {Find out how many records there are}
    NoOfCentres :=  DummyCentre.CentreNumber;
    If NoOfCentres > 0
      Then
        For Count := 1 To NoOfCentres
          Do Read (CentreFile,Centre[Count]);
    CloseFile(CentreFile);
```

```
{Load Candidate file}
AssignFile (CandidateFile, CandidateFileName);
Reset (CandidateFile);
Read (CandidateFile, DummyCandidate);
{Find out how many records there are}
NoOfCandidates :=  DummyCandidate.CentreNumber;
If NoOfCandidates > 0
  Then
    For Count := 1 To NoOfCandidates
      Do Read (CandidateFile,Candidate[Count]);
CloseFile(CandidateFile);


{Load Request File}
AssignFile (RequestFile, RequestFileName);
Reset (RequestFile);
Read (RequestFile, DummyRequest);
{Find out how many records there are}
NoOfRequests :=  DummyRequest.CentreNumber;
If NoOfRequests > 0
  Then
    For Count := 1 To NoOfRequests
      Do Read (RequestFile,Request[Count]);
CloseFile(RequestFile);
End;


Procedure SaveFiles;
Var
  Count : Integer;
  DummyRequest : TRequest;
  DummyCentre: TCentre;
  DummyCandidate : TCandidate;
Begin
  {Save Centre Records}
  AssignFile (CentreFile, CentreFileName);
  ReWrite (CentreFile);
  DummyCentre.CentreNumber := NoOfCentres;
  {update number of records in Dummy record}
  Write (CentreFile, DummyCentre);
  If NoOfCentres > 0
    Then
      For Count := 1 To NoOfCentres
        Do Write (CentreFile,Centre[Count]);
  CloseFile(CentreFile);
```

```
{Save Candidate Records}
AssignFile (CandidateFile, CandidateFileName);
ReWrite (CandidateFile);
DummyCandidate.CentreNumber := NoOfCandidates;
{update number of records in Dummy record}
Write (CandidateFile, DummyCandidate);
If NoOfCandidates > 0
  Then
    For Count := 1 To NoOfCandidates
    Do Write (CandidateFile,Candidate[Count]);
CloseFile(CandidateFile);


{Save Request Records}
AssignFile (RequestFile, RequestFileName);
ReWrite (RequestFile);
DummyRequest.CentreNumber := NoOfRequests;
{update number of request records in Dummy record}
Write (RequestFile, DummyRequest);
If NoOfRequests > 0
  Then
    For Count := 1 To NoOfRequests
      Do Write (RequestFile,Request[Count]);
CloseFile(RequestFile);
End;


{*********** Other routines *********************}


Function Hash (S : String) : Byte; {Hashing Algorithm}
Var
  V, Dummy : Integer;
  Begin
    S := MidStr(S,4,2); {get last 2 digits of Ref Code}
    Val(S, V, Dummy);   {Change S into equivalent number}
    Hash := V;
  End;


Procedure InitialisePrinter;
  Begin
    Assignprn (Output); {assign default printer to text file}
    Rewrite (Output);
    Printer.Canvas.Font.Name := 'Courier New';
    Printer.Canvas.Font.Size := 14;
  End;
```

```pascal
Function LookupGrade(SubjectRefCode:String ; Mark:Byte): Char;
Var
  Pos : LongInt;
  Grade : Char;
  Begin
    Assignfile (SubjectFile,'UKABSubjects.dat');
    Reset (SubjectFile);
    Pos := Hash (SubjectRefCode);
    Seek (SubjectFile, Pos);
    Read (SubjectFile, Subject);
    CloseFile (SubjectFile);
    Grade := 'A';
    While (Subject.Boundary[Grade] > Mark) And (Grade < 'F')
      Do Grade := Succ(Grade);
    If Grade = 'F'
      Then Grade := 'U';
    LookupGrade := Grade;
End;


Function AllDigits (X: String) : Boolean;
Var
  L, P : Integer;
  OK : Boolean;
  Begin
    OK := True;
    L := Length (X);
    For P := 1 To L
      Do
        If (MidStr(X,P,1) < '0') Or (MidStr(X,P,1) > '9')
          Then OK := False;
    AllDigits := OK;
  End;


Function GetValidCandNo : String;
Var
  Temp: String;
  Valid : Boolean;
  Begin
    Repeat
      Write ('Candidate Number:  '); Readln (Temp);
      Valid := (Length(Temp) = 4) And AllDigits (Temp);
      If Not Valid
        Then Writeln ('Candidate Number must have 4 digits.');
    Until Valid;
    GetValidCandNo := Temp;
  End;
```

```
Function GetValidCentreNo : Integer;
Var
  Temp : String;
  Valid : Boolean;
  Value, Code : Integer;
  Begin
    Repeat
      Write ('Centre Number: '); Readln(Temp);
      Valid := (Length(Temp) = 5) And AllDigits (Temp);
      If Valid
        Then
          Begin
            Val(Temp, Value, Code);
            Valid := (Value >= 10000) And (Value <= 80000);
          End;
      If Not Valid
        Then Writeln ('Centre Number must be betw 10000 and 80000');
    Until Valid;
    GetValidCentreNo := Value;
  End;


Function GetValidSubjectRefCode : String;
Var
  Temp : String;
  Valid : Boolean;
  Pos : Integer;
  Begin
    AssignFile (SubjectFile, 'UKABSubjects.dat');
    Reset (SubjectFile);
    Repeat
      Write ('Subject Reference Code: '); Readln (Temp);
      Valid := (Length(Temp) = 5 ) And AllDigits (Temp);
      If Valid
        Then
          Begin
            Pos := Hash (Temp);
            Seek (SubjectFile, Pos);
            Read (SubjectFile, Subject);
            Valid := Subject.SubjectRefCode = Temp;
          End;
      If Not Valid
        Then Writeln ('Subject Ref Code must be 5 digits.');
    Until Valid;
    CloseFile (SubjectFile);
    GetValidSubjectRefCode := Temp;
  End;
```

```pascal
Function GetValidMark : Byte;
Var
  Temp : String;
  Valid : Boolean;
  Value, Dummy : Integer;
  Begin
    Repeat
      Write ('Original Mark: '); Readln (Temp);
      Valid := (AllDigits (Temp)) And (Length(Temp)>0);
      If Valid
        Then
          Begin
            Val (Temp, Value, Dummy);
            Valid := (Value >=0) And (Value <= 100);
          End;
      If Not Valid
        Then Writeln ('Marks must be between 0 and 100');
    Until Valid;
    GetValidMark := Value;
  End;


Function PointerToRequest : Integer;
Var
  Found, NotThere : Boolean;
  Pointer, CentreNumber : Integer;
  CandidateNumber, SubjectRefCode: String[5];
  Begin
    CandidateNumber := GetValidCandNo;
    CentreNumber := GetValidCentreNo;
    SubjectRefCode := GetValidSubjectRefCode;
    Found:= False; Pointer := 0;
    Repeat
      Pointer := Pointer + 1;
      If (Request[Pointer].CandidateNumber = CandidateNumber)
        And (Request[Pointer].CentreNumber = CentreNumber)
        And (Request[Pointer].SubjectRefCode = SubjectRefCode)
        Then Found := True;
      NotThere := (Pointer = NoOfRequests) And Not Found;
    Until Found Or NotThere;
    If NotThere
      Then
        Begin
          Writeln ('Sorry this request does not exist');
          Pointer := 0;
        End;
    PointerToRequest := Pointer;
  End;
```

```
Procedure CheckCentre (CentreNo: Integer);
Var
  Found, NotThere : Boolean;
  Pointer : Integer;
  Begin
    Found := False; Pointer := 0;
    If NoOfCentres = 0
      Then NotThere := True
      Else
        Repeat
          Pointer := Pointer + 1;
          If (Centre[Pointer].CentreNumber = CentreNo)
            Then Found := True;
          NotThere := (Pointer = NoOfCentres) And Not Found;
        Until Found Or NotThere;
    If NotThere
      Then
        Begin
          NoOfCentres := NoOfCentres + 1;
          Centre[NoOfCentres].CentreNumber := CentreNo;
          Write ('Centre Address: ');
          Readln (Centre[NoOfCentres].CentreAddress);
        End;
  End;


Function UniqueRequest (CentreNo: Integer; CandNo, Subject: String): Boolean;
Var
  Pointer: Integer;
  NotThere, Found : Boolean;
  Begin
    Pointer := 0;
    Found := False;
    {no need to check for duplicates if no requests exist}
    If NoOfRequests > 0
      Then
        Repeat
          Pointer := Pointer + 1;
          If (Request[Pointer].CentreNumber = CentreNo)
              And (Request[Pointer].CandidateNumber = CandNo)
              And (Request[Pointer].SubjectRefCode = Subject)
            Then Found := True;
          NotThere := (Pointer = NoOfRequests) And Not Found;
        Until Found Or NotThere;
    UniqueRequest := Not Found;
  End;
```

```
Procedure CheckCandidate (CentreNo: Integer; CandNo: String);
Var
  Found, NotThere : Boolean;
  Pointer : Integer;
  Begin
    Found:= False; Pointer := 0;
    If NoOfCandidates = 0
      Then NotThere := True
      Else
        Repeat
          Pointer := Pointer + 1;
          If (Candidate[Pointer].CentreNumber = CentreNo)
              And (Candidate[Pointer].CandidateNumber = CandNo)
            Then Found := True;
          NotThere := (Pointer = NoOfCandidates) And Not Found;
        Until Found Or NotThere;
    If NotThere
      Then
        Begin
          NoOfCandidates := NoOfCandidates + 1;
          Candidate[NoOfCandidates].CandidateNumber := CandNo;
          Candidate[NoOfCandidates].CentreNumber := CentreNo;
          Write ('Candidate Name: ');
          Readln (Candidate[NoOfCandidates].CandidateName);
        End;
  End;
```

Q 4 (b)

```
Procedure ShowCompleteRecord (Pointer : Integer);
Begin
  With Request[Pointer]
    Do
      Begin
        Writeln;
        Writeln('Date request received:  ',DateTimeToStr(DateRequest));
        Writeln('Centre Number:          ', CentreNumber);
        Writeln('Candidate Number:       ', CandidateNumber);
        Writeln('Subject Reference Code: ', SubjectRefCode);
        Writeln('Original Mark/ Grade:   ',OrigMark,'  ', OrigGrade);
        Writeln('Re-mark Mark / Grade:   ', ReMark, '  ', ReGrade);
        Write  ('Re-mark received:       ');
        If DateRemark > 0
          Then Writeln(DateTimeToStr(DateRemark))
          Else Writeln;
        Write ('Script return:          ');
        If ScriptReturn
          Then Writeln ('Yes')
          Else Writeln ('No');
      End;
End;
```

```
{***************** Menu Options **************************}


Procedure NewRequest;
Var
  Response: Char;
  ValidRequest: Boolean;
  Begin
    ValidRequest := False;
    With Request[NoOfRequests+1]
      Do
        Begin
          CentreNumber := GetValidCentreNo;
          CheckCentre (CentreNumber);
          CandidateNumber := GetValidCandNo ;
          CheckCandidate (CentreNumber, CandidateNumber);
          SubjectRefCode := GetValidSubjectrefCode;
          If UniqueRequest (CentreNumber, CandidateNumber, SubjectRefCode)
            Then
              Begin
                ValidRequest := True;
                {only continue if valid request}
                OrigMark := GetValidMark;
                DateRequest := Date;
                OrigGrade:= LookupGrade(SubjectRefCode, OrigMark);
              End;
        End;
    If ValidRequest
      Then
        Begin
          Write ('Script to be returned? Y/N: '); Readln (Response);
          Request[NoOfRequests+1].ScriptReturn := Response = 'Y';
          ShowCompleteRecord (NoOfRequests+1);
          Write ('Save this record? Y/N '); Readln (Response);
          If Response = 'Y'
            Then NoOfRequests := NoOfRequests + 1; {accept record}
        End
      Else Writeln ('Not a unique request. Please check your details.');
  End;
```

```pascal
Procedure DeleteRequest;
Var
  Pointer, Count : Integer;
  Response: Char;
  Begin
    Pointer := PointerToRequest;   {get pointer to wanted record}
    If Pointer > 0
      Then {record was found}
        Begin{Check this is the correct record to be deleted}
          ShowCompleteRecord (Pointer);
          Write ('Is this the record you wish to delete? Y/N ');
          Readln (Response);
          If Response = 'Y'
            Then {shuffle up the entries following the obsolete one}
              Begin
                For Count := Pointer to NoOfRequests-1
                  Do Request[Count] := Request[Count+1];
                NoOfRequests := NoOfRequests - 1;
              End;
        End;
  End;


Procedure EnterRemark;
Var
  Pointer : Integer;
  Response : Char;
  Begin
    Pointer := PointerToRequest;
    If Pointer > 0
      Then
        Begin {Record found}
          ShowCompleteRecord (Pointer);
          Write ('Is this the record you wish to update? Y/N ');
          Readln (Response);
          If Response = 'Y'
            Then
              Begin
                Write ('Enter new mark: '); {Need to validate}
                With Request[Pointer]
                  Do
                    Begin
                      Readln (ReMark);
                      Regrade := LookupGrade(SubjectRefCode,ReMark);
                      DateRemark := Date;
                    End;
              End;
        End;
  End;
```

```
Function CentreAddress (CentreNo: Integer) : String;
Var  Count : Integer;
  Begin
    Count := 0;
    Repeat
      Count := Count + 1;
    Until Centre[Count].CentreNumber  = CentreNo;
    CentreAddress :=  Centre[Count].CentreAddress;
  End;


Procedure GradeChanges;
Var  Count : Integer;
  Begin
    InitialisePrinter;
    Printer.Canvas.Font.Style := [fsBold];
    Write (Output, '  Today''s Remarks resulting in Grade Changes ');
    Writeln (Output, DateToStr(Date));
    Writeln (Output, '
=====================================================');
    Writeln (Output);
    Printer.Canvas.Font.Style := [];
    Write (Output, 'Date':6, 'Centre':13, 'Candidate':11);
    Write (Output, 'Subject':9, 'Orig.':7, 'Orig.':6);
    Writeln (Output, 'Remark':8, 'New':4);
    Write (Output, 'Requested':11, 'Number':8, 'Number':8);
    Write (Output,'Ref Code':13, 'Mark':5, 'Grade':7);
    Writeln (Output, 'Mark':6, 'Grade':7);
    For Count := 1 To NoOfRequests
      Do
        If  (Request[Count].OrigGrade <> Request[Count].ReGrade)
            And (Request[Count].DateRemark = Date)
          Then
            Begin
              Write (Output, DateTimeToStr(Request[Count].DateRequest):12);
              Write (Output, Request[Count].CentreNumber:7);
              Write (Output, Request[Count].CandidateNumber:6);
              Write (Output, request[Count].SubjectRefCode:12);
              Write (Output, Request[Count].OrigMark:6);
              Write (Output, Request[Count].OrigGrade:5);
              Write (Output, Request[Count].ReMark:8);
              Writeln (Output, Request[Count].ReGrade:6);
            End;
    Close (Output);
  End;
```

```
Function CandName (CentreNo: Integer; CandNo: String) : String;
Var
  Count : Integer;
  Begin
    Count := 0;
    Repeat
      Count := Count + 1;
    Until (Candidate[Count].CentreNumber  = CentreNo)
      And (Candidate[Count].CandidateNumber = CandNo);
    CandName :=  Candidate[Count].CandidateName;
  End;


Procedure PrintListOutstanding;
Var
  Count : Integer;
  Begin
    InitialisePrinter;
    Printer.Canvas.Font.Style := [fsBold];
    Write (Output, '  Requests outstanding after 3 weeks as on ');
    Writeln (Output, DateToStr(Date));
    Writeln (Output, '  =================================================');
    Writeln (Output);
    Printer.Canvas.Font.Style := [];
    Write (Output, 'Date':6, 'Centre':14, 'Candidate':11);
    Writeln (Output, 'Subject':9, 'Original':11, 'Original':11);
    Write (Output, 'Requested':11, 'Number':9, 'Number':8);
    Writeln (Output, 'Ref Code':13, 'Mark':6, 'Grade':12);
    For Count := 1 To NoOfRequests
      Do
        If (Request[Count].DateRemark =0)
          And (Request[Count].DateRequest < Date-21)      Q2 (a) (iii)
          Then
            Begin
              Write (Output,DateTimeToStr(Request[Count].DateRequest):12);
              Write (Output,Request[Count].CentreNumber:7);
              Write (Output,Request[Count].CandidateNumber:7);
              Write (Output,Request[Count].SubjectRefCode:12);
              Write (Output,Request[Count].OrigMark:7);
              Writeln (Output, Request[Count].OrigGrade:10);
            End;
    Close (Output);
  End;
```

```
Procedure SubjectList;
Var
   Count : Integer;
   SubjectRefCode: String[5];
   Begin
      InitialisePrinter;
      Printer.Canvas.Font.Style := [fsBold];
      SubjectRefCode := GetValidSubjectRefCode;
      Write (Output, '  Requests by Subject Ref Code ', SubjectrefCode, '  ');
      Writeln (Output, DateToStr(Date));
      Writeln (Output, '  ===========================================');
      Writeln (Output);
      Printer.Canvas.Font.Style := [];
      Write (Output, 'Date':6, 'Centre':14, 'Candidate':11, 'Original':10);
      Writeln (Output, 'Original':10, 'Remark':8, 'New':5);
      Write (Output, 'Requested':11, 'Number':9, 'Number':8);
      Writeln (Output, 'Mark':9, 'Grade':11, 'Mark':9, 'Grade':9);
      For Count := 1 To NoOfRequests
         Do
            If  Request[Count].SubjectRefCode = SubjectRefCode
               Then
                  Begin
                     Write (Output, DateTimeToStr(Request[Count].DateRequest):12);
                     Write (Output, Request[Count].CentreNumber:7);
                     Write (Output, Request[Count].CandidateNumber:7);
                     Write (Output, Request[Count].OrigMark:9);
                     Write (Output, Request[Count].OrigGrade:9);
                     If  Request[Count].DateReMark > 0
                        Then
                           Begin
                              Write (Output, Request[Count].ReMark:11);
                              Writeln (Output, Request[Count].ReGrade:7);
                           End
                        Else Writeln(Output);
                  End;
      Close (Output);
   End;
```

Q2(a)(i)

```
Procedure CentreList;
Var
  Count, CentreNumber: Integer;
  Begin
    InitialisePrinter;
    Printer.Canvas.Font.Style := [fsBold];
    CentreNumber := GetValidCentreNo;
    Write (Output, '  Requests by Centre ', CentreNumber, '   ');
    Writeln (Output, DateToStr(Date));
    Writeln (Output, '  ======================================');
    Writeln (Output);
    Printer.Canvas.Font.Style := [];
    Write (Output, 'Date':6, 'Candidate':16, 'Subject':9);
    Writeln (Output, 'Original':11, 'Original':10, 'Remark':7, 'New':5);
    Write (Output, 'Requested':11, 'Number':8,'Ref Code':13);
    Writeln (Output, 'Mark':6, 'Grade':11, 'Mark':8, 'Grade':9);
    For Count := 1 To NoOfRequests
      Do
        If  Request[Count].CentreNumber = CentreNumber
          Then
            Begin
              Write (Output, DateTimeToStr(Request[Count].DateRequest):12);
              Write (Output, Request[Count].CandidateNumber:5);
              Write (Output, Request[Count].SubjectRefCode:12);
              Write (Output, Request[Count].OrigMark:7);
              Write (Output, Request[Count].OrigGrade:10);
              If  Request[Count].DateReMark > 0
                Then
                  Begin
                    Write (Output, Request[Count].ReMark:9);
                    Writeln (Output, Request[Count].ReGrade:7);
                  End
                Else Writeln(Output);
            End;
    Close (Output);
  End;
```

```
Procedure LetterToCentre;
Var
  Count : Integer;
  Pointer : LongInt;
  Response : Char;
  Begin
    Pointer := PointerToRequest;
    If Pointer > 0
      Then
        Begin {Record found}
          ShowCompleteRecord (Pointer);
          Write ('Is this the result you wish to send Y/N?  ');
          Readln (Response);
          If Response = 'Y'
            Then
              Begin
                InitialisePrinter;
                Printer.Canvas.Font.Style := [fsBold];
                For Count := 1 To 15   {empty lines for letterhead}
                  Do Writeln (Output);
                Write (Output, '  Centre Number : ');
                Writeln (Output, Request[Pointer].CentreNumber);
                Write (Output, '  Centre Address: ');
                Writeln (Output,CentreAddress(Request[Pointer].CentreNumber));
                Writeln (Output, DateToStr(Date):60);
                Writeln (Output, '  Result of remark request');
                Writeln (Output, '  =======================');
                Writeln (Output);
                Printer.Canvas.Font.Style := [];
                Write (Output, 'Candidate':11, 'Candidate':11, 'Subject':21);
                Writeln (Output, 'Original':11, 'Original':10);
                Write (Output, 'Number':8, 'Name':9, 'Ref Code':27);
                Writeln (Output, 'Mark':6, 'Grade':11);
                With Request[Pointer] Do
                  Begin
                    Write (Output, CandidateNumber:6,'          ');
                    Write (Output,CandName(CentreNumber, CandidateNumber):21);
                    Write (Output, SubjectRefCode:7);
                    Write (Output, OrigMark:7);
                    Writeln (Output, OrigGrade:9);
                    Writeln (Output);
                    If  ReMark <> OrigMark
                      Then
                        Begin
                          Write (Output, '  The revised number of marks is ');
                          Writeln (Output, ReMark:4,'.');
```

```
                            If OrigGrade <> ReGrade
                              Then
                                Begin
                                  Write (Output, '  Revised grade: ');
                                  Writeln (Output, ReGrade:2);
                                End
                              Else
                              Writeln (Output, '  No change of grade.');
                            End
                          Else Writeln(Output, '  No change to marks or grade');
                    End;
                End;
                Close (Output);
        End;
  End;


Procedure ListRecords;
Var
  Count : Integer;
  Begin
    Writeln ('No of Centres: ', NoOfCentres);
    Writeln ('No of Candidates: ', NoOfCandidates);
    Writeln ('No of Requests: ', NoOfRequests);
    For Count := 1 To NoOfCentres
      Do
        Writeln (Centre[Count].CentreNumber,' ', Centre[Count].CentreAddress);
    For Count := 1 To NoOfCandidates
     Do
       With Candidate[Count]
         Do
           Writeln ( CentreNumber,' ',CandidateNumber, '  ',CandidateName);
    For Count := 1 To NoOfRequests
      Do
        With Request[Count]
          Do
            Begin
              Write ({CandidateName:25,} CentreNumber:6, CandidateNumber:5);
              Write (SubjectRefCode:6, OrigMark:3, OrigGrade:2, ReMark:3);
              Write (ReGrade:2,ScriptReturn:6, DateTimeToStr(DateRequest):11);
              If DateRemark > 0
                Then Writeln (DateTimeToStr(DateRemark):11)
                Else Writeln;
            End;
  End;
```

```
Function Option: Integer;
Var
  Response : Integer;
  Begin
    Writeln;
    Writeln;
    Writeln;
    Writeln ('     UKAB Remark Service');
    Writeln ('     ===================');
    Writeln;
    Writeln ('     Please choose an option ');
    Writeln;
    Writeln ('     1 - New Request');
    Writeln ('     2 - Delete Request');
    Writeln ('     3 - Enter Remark');
    Writeln ('     4 - Daily List of Grade Changes');
    Writeln ('     5 - Daily List of Outstanding Re-Marks');
    Writeln ('     6 - Subject List');
    Writeln ('     7 - Centre List');
    Writeln ('     8 - Letter to Centre');
    Writeln ('     9 - List records on screen');
    Writeln ('    10 - Exit Program');
    Writeln;
    Write    ('     Enter Option Number: '); Readln (Response);
    Option := Response
  End;
```

```pascal
{******************* Main Program Body ***************************}

Begin
  LoadFiles;
  Finished := False;
  Repeat
    Case Option Of
      1: NewRequest;
      2: DeleteRequest;
      3: EnterRemark;
      4: GradeChanges;
      5: PrintListOutstanding;
      6: SubjectList;
      7: CentreList;
      8: LetterToCentre;
      9: ListRecords;
      10: Finished := True;
      Else Writeln ('Please enter a valid Option Number');
    End;
  Until Finished;
  SaveFiles;
End.
```

Selected questions with answers from the AQA May 2003 Examination paper for Unit 3 (CPT3)

Question 2

This question relates to the IMPLEMENTATION process.
(a) In order to produce the requested hard copy lists, your solution has to find certain records. Exactly how did your solution find:
  (i) records where re-marks have been requested for a particular subject;

> The program searches through all requests held, and compares the subject code with the Subject Reference Code for the particular subject.

(2 marks)

Where in your documentation is your coding to find this data?

Page number   P-39

(1 mark)

(Write Q2(a)(i) in the margin, in the correct place, on that page.)

  (ii) records where the candidate's mark has changed causing a change in grade;

> The record storing the request details has fields for both the original grade and the re-mark grade. The program searches through all completed requests held, and compares the original grade with the re-mark grade

(2 marks)

Where is a hard copy of such a list in your documentation?
Page number   P-17

(1 mark)

(Write Q2(a)(ii) in the margin, in the correct place, on that page.)

  (iii) records where re-marks have not been completed in the required three-week period?

> I stored the date on which the re-mark was done, so I can check where this date is not filled in and the date the request was received is more than 21 days from 'today'.

(3 marks)

Give the page number either of the coding to produce this list or a hard copy of this list in your documentation.

Page number   P-38   *(1 mark)*

(Write Q 2(a)(iii) in the margin, in the correct place, on that page.)

(b)   You were asked to produce a daily list of those re-marks where the candidate's grade has been affected by a mark change. UKAB decides it also needs a daily list of those re-marks where the grade has not changed, whether or not the mark had been changed.

Write an algorithm to produce this list.

```
For each request do
    If re-mark date = today's date
        AND original grade = re-mark grade
        Then print out re-mark details
    Endif
End loop
```

(5 marks)

Total marks 15

Question 3

This question relates to the REPORT DESIGN process.

(a) (i) On which page of your documentation is a hard copy of the document to be returned to centres, complete with UKAB logo?

Page number   *P-19*   *(1 mark)*

(Write Q3(a)(i) in the margin, in the correct place, on that page.)

(ii) How did you input the logo and position it on this document?

I scanned in the logo from the specification and placed it in an empty word-processed document and printed it to make pre-printed stationery. I had to make sure when printing the document that I left enough empty lines not to print over the letterhead.   *(3 marks)*

(b) Give two criteria that you have considered for the design of this document, other than using the logo, and say how you have used each of them.

1 Easy to read information – used bold type for centre details, underlined purpose of document.
2 Layout easy to follow – heading carefully lined up over the data.   *(4 marks)*

(Write Q 3(b) in the margin of your document, in the correct place(s) on the page(s), where these two aspects of design are demonstrated.)

(2 marks)
Total marks 10

Question 4

This question relates to the TESTING and VALIDATION process.

(a) How did your solution prevent the entry of a mark greater than 100?

> When the program asks for the original mark it will only move to the next question if a number between 0 and 100 is typed in.

(1 mark)

(b) How did you ensure that your solution would allow two candidates with the same candidate number but from different centres?

> I used test data of two candidates with the same number from different centres doing the same subject. So the candidate numbers and subject reference codes were the same but the centre numbers were different.

(2 marks)

Where is this made clear in your documentation?

Page number   P-34

(1 mark)

(Write Q4(b) in the margin, in the correct place, on that page.)

(c) What test data did you use for a candidate's mark being
   (i) increased;   original mark 70, new mark 73
   (ii) decreased?   original mark 66, new mark 59

(2 marks)

Where is the evidence of this testing in your documentation?

Page number   P-20   And   P-17

(2 marks)

(Write Q 4(c)(i) and 4 (c)(ii) in the margin, in the correct places, on those pages.)

Total marks 8

Chapter 25 – Solution using Delphi

The following pages contain the documentation for a model answer for the 2003 Practical Exercise. On pages *D-35* to *D-38* are selected questions from the AQA May 2003 question paper with answers, including the reference to evidence from the following documentation.

Analysis

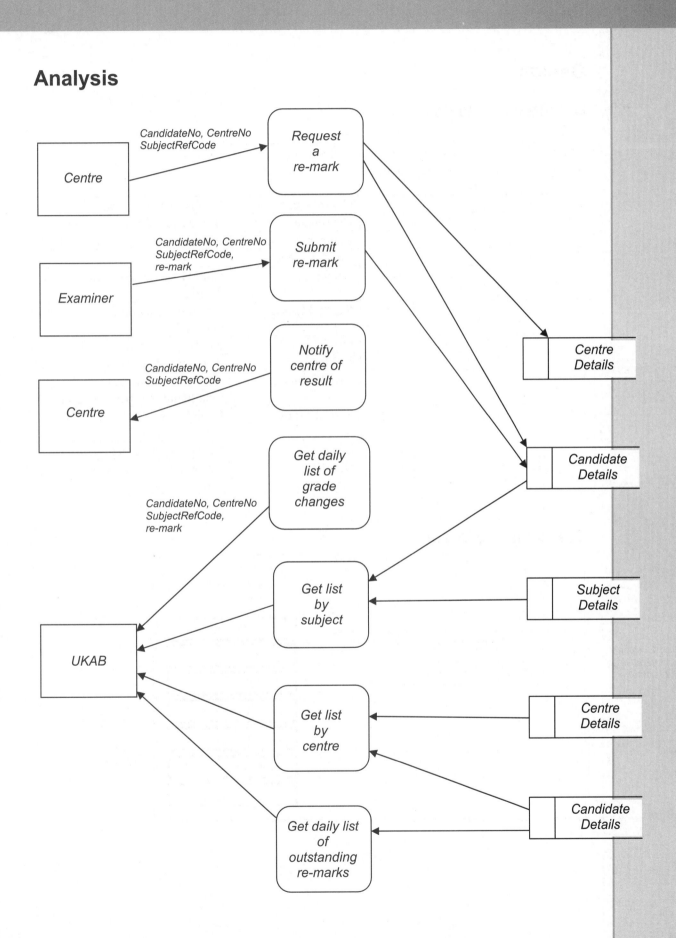

Design

Data Requirements

Required by specification	Required on document to centre	Extra fields	Field Name	Notes
Y	Y		CentreNumber	Unique when combined
Y	Y		CandidateNumber	(Centre could ask for re-mark of
Y	Y		SubjectRefCode	several subjects for same candidate)
Y	Y		CandidateName	
	Y		OrigGrade	Could be **calculated** from subject details
	Y		ReMarkGrade	Could be **calculated** from subject details
Y	Y		OrigMark	whole number between 1 and 100
Y	Y		ReMark	whole number between 1 and 100
Y			GradeBoundary	Need this for A, B, C, D, E (whole number between 1 and 100)
Y			ScriptReturn	Boolean, whether centre requested return of script
		Y	DateRemark	Needed to determine daily list
		Y	DateRequest	Needed to determine outstanding re-marks

User Interface Design

Note: *This could be hand-drawn on a separate page*

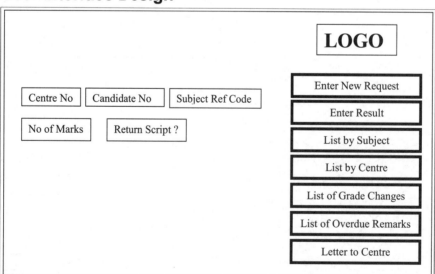

Printed Output Design

```
Requests by Subject Ref Code xxxxx  xx/xx/xxxxx
===================================================

Date         Centre   Candidate Original Original Remark New
Requested    Number   Number    Mark     Grade    Mark   Grade
xx/xx/xxxx   xxxxx    xxxx      xx       X        xx     X
```

```
Today's Remarks resulting in Grade Changes  xx/xx/xxxxx
=========================================================

Date         Centre   Candidate Subject   Orig. Orig.  Remark New
Requested    Number   Number    Ref Code  Mark  Grade  Mark   Grade
xx/xx/xxxx   xxxxx    xxxx      xxxxx     xx    X      xx     X
```

```
Requests by Centre xxxx  xx/xx/xxxxx
===================================

Date         Candidate Subject   Original Original Remark New
Requested    Number    Ref Code  Mark     Grade    Mark   Grade
xx/xx/xxxx   xxxxx     xxxxx     xx       X        xx     X
```

Chosen Font:
Courier New
Size: 14

Letter to Centre (leave enough space for letter head, 15 lines):

Chosen Font:
Courier New
Size: 14

```
Centre Number : xxxxx


                                          xx/xx/xxxx

Result of remark request
=========================

Candidate Candidate                Subject  Original Original
Number    Name                     Ref Code Mark     Grade
xxxx      xxxxxxxxxxxxxxxxxxxxxxxxx xxxxx    xx       X

No changes to marks or grade

Or

The revised number of marks is  xx.
No change of grade.

Or

The revised number of marks is  xx.
Revised grade:  X.
```

Record Structure and Table Design

Subject

Field Name	Data Type	Length	Validation	Comment
SubjectRefCode	Text	5	5 digits, must exist	Unique (key)
A	Byte			Stores boundary mark for respective grades
B	Byte			
C	Byte			
D	Byte			
E	Byte			

Candidate

Field Name	Data Type	Length	Validation	Comment
CentreNo	Integer		Between 10000 and 80000	Composite key (CandidateNumber unique to Centre)
CandidateNo	Text	4	4 digits	
CandidateName	Text	25		

Request

Field Name	Data Type	Length	Validation	Comment
CentreNo	Integer		Must exist in Candidate table	Unique (Composite key)
CandidateNo	Text	4		
SubjectRefCode	Text	5	Must exist in Subject table	
OrigMark	Byte		Between 0 and 100	
ReMark	Byte		Between 0 and 100	
OrigGrade	Text	1	Looked up from Subject table	
ReGrade	Text	1	Looked up from Subject table	
ScriptReturn	Boolean			Only one of two possible values
DateRequest	Date		System date	Today's date when request is entered into system
DateRemark	Date		System date	Today's date when remark is entered into system

Testplan

make up 15 candidates
make up 4 centres
make up requests (about 20 requests)

must have the following cases:

remarks more than original mark
remark less than original mark

no change in grade
change in grade

1 or more requests from a centre
0, 1 or more requests per subject

requests outstanding after 3 weeks

extra:
candidates with remarks for several subjects

Test Number	Test Type	Evidence Page Number
1	Validation of centre number	11
2	Validation of candidate number	11
3	Validation of subject reference code	11
4	Validation of marks	11
5	Correct grade is looked up	12
6	Unique request	12
7	List of requests by subject reference code	13
8	List of requests by centre	14
9	Daily list of grade changes	15
10	Daily list of outstanding re-marks	16
11	Document to centre no change to marks or grade	17
12	Document to centre no change to grade	18
13	Document to centre with grade change	19

Candidate Name	Centre Number	Cand. Number	Subject Ref Code	Orig. Marks	Grade*	re-mark Marks	Grade*	grade change*	Script return?	Date remark was requested*	Date script was remarked*	Reason for choice
Mickey Mouse	12345	2345	54821	45	U	55	E	Y	Y	26-Mar-03	27-Mar-03	E borderline after re-mark
Jimmy Nail	12345	4556	54821	84	B	85	A	Y	Y	26-Mar-03	31-Mar-03	more than one candidate from this centre
Jack Sprat	12345	7799	01325	47	U	51	E		Y	26-Mar-03	31-Mar-03	1 mark off an E before re-mark
Oliver Twist	22151	1001	54821	70	D	73	D		Y	26-Mar-03	31-Mar-03	1 mark off a C after re-mark
Joe Bloggs	22151	1234	01325	58	D	55	D			26-Mar-03	31-Mar-03	
Joe Bloggs	22151	1234	20094	35	E	32	E			26-Mar-03	31-Mar-03	more than one subject from this candidate
Joe Bloggs	22151	1234	28181	40	U				Y	26-Mar-03		overdue
Joe Bloggs	22151	1234	54821	50	U	49	U			26-Mar-03	31-Mar-03	
Chris Evans	22151	4455	54821	76	C	80	B	Y		26-Mar-03	31-Mar-03	grade change up
Tom Thumb	22151	4567	01325	66	C	59	D	Y	Y	26-Mar-03	31-Mar-03	grade change down
Jemima Spratt	22151	5678	01325	99	A	100	A			26-Mar-03	31-Mar-03	extreme marks
Anna Karenina	22151	6789	01325	0	U	0	U			26-Mar-03	31-Mar-03	extreme marks
Anna Karenina	22151	6789	54821	63	E				Y	26-Mar-03		overdue
Violet Day	22151	7456	54821	72	D					26-Mar-03		overdue
Fred Flintstone	23456	2222	54821	84	B	85	A	Y	Y	26-Mar-03	31-Mar-03	1 centre 1 request, borderline A after re-mark
Rose Budd	77777	0100	28181	65	D					26-Mar-03		overdue, leading zero in Cand. No.
Donald Duck	77777	1234	54821	47	U					26-Mar-03		same CandNo as centre 22151
Jack Russell	80000	3456	28181	50	E					26-Mar-03		overdue, centre No extreme
Jack Russell	10000	3456	54821	19	U					26-Mar-03		overdue, centre No. extreme

Candidate Name	Centre Number	Cand. Number	Subject Ref Code	Orig. Marks	Grade*	re-mark Marks	Grade*	grade change*	Script return?	Date remark was requested*	Date script was remarked*	Reason for choice
Jimmy Nail	12345	4556	93421	34					Y	26-Mar-03		wrong subject code, but hashes to a subject record
	80001											invalid centre number
	9999											invalid centre number
	abcde											invalid centre number
	empty string											no centre number entered
		234										invalid candidate number
		34567										invalid candidate number
		abc										invalid candidate number
		empty string										no candidate number
			abcde									invalid subject code
			3421									invalid subject code
			933421									invalid subject code
			empty string									no subject code
				-1								invalid marks
				101								invalid marks
				empty string								no marks
				a								invalid marks

* means data not entered, but calculated by program, just in table for checking

bold are those entries I expect to see in lists by centre (22151), subject ref code (54821), grade changes (25/3/03),

Overdue (on and after 10/4/03)

Testing

Tip: *Be sure to capture the whole window showing the error message and the data that causd it.*

Test		
1	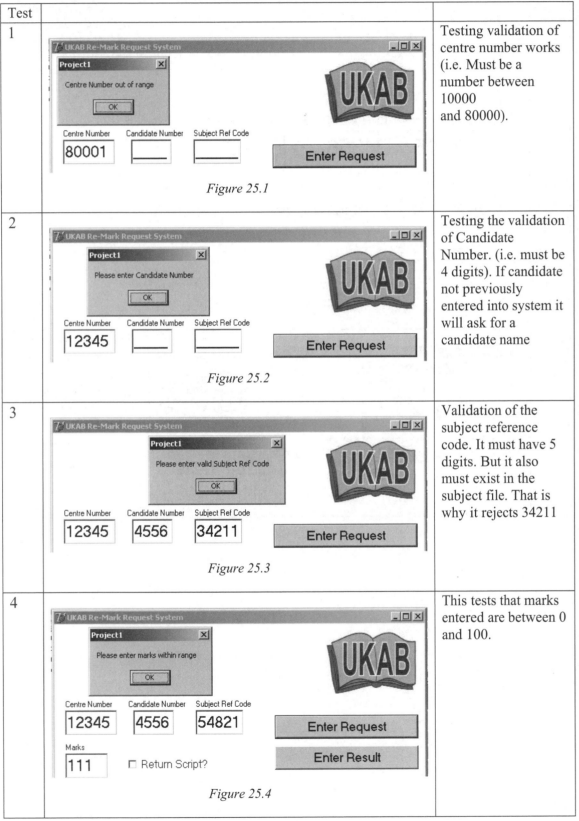 *Figure 25.1*	Testing validation of centre number works (i.e. Must be a number between 10000 and 80000).
2	*Figure 25.2*	Testing the validation of Candidate Number. (i.e. must be 4 digits). If candidate not previously entered into system it will ask for a candidate name
3	*Figure 25.3*	Validation of the subject reference code. It must have 5 digits. But it also must exist in the subject file. That is why it rejects 34211
4	*Figure 25.4*	This tests that marks entered are between 0 and 100.

5	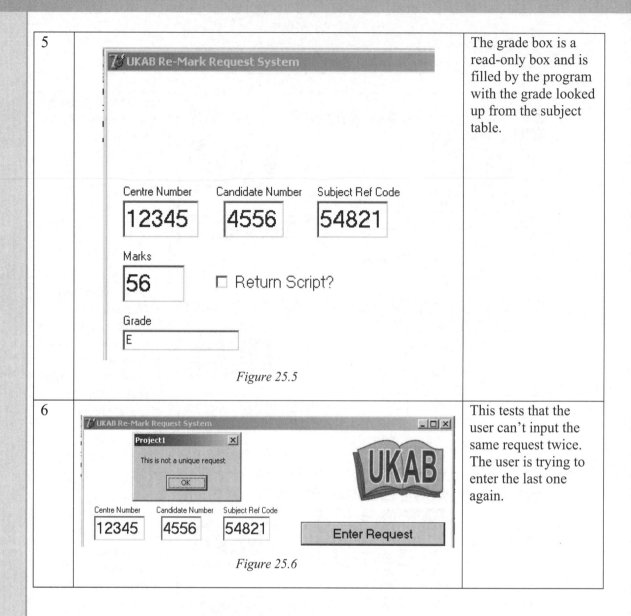 Figure 25.5	The grade box is a read-only box and is filled by the program with the grade looked up from the subject table.
6	Figure 25.6	This tests that the user can't input the same request twice. The user is trying to enter the last one again.

Requests by Subject Ref Code 54821   31/03/2003

===

Date Requested	Centre Number	Candidate Number	Original Mark	Original Grade	Remark Mark	New Grade
26/03/2003	12345	2345	45	U	55	E
26/03/2003	12345	4556	84	B	85	A
26/03/2003	22151	1001	70	D	73	D
26/03/2003	22151	1234	50	U	49	U
26/03/2003	22151	4455	76	C	80	B
26/03/2003	22151	6789	63	E		
26/03/2003	22151	7456	72	D		
26/03/2003	23456	2222	84	B	85	A
26/03/2003	77777	1234	47	U		
26/03/2003	10000	3456	19	U		

Q1(a)(ii)

Note: This is evidence for Qi(a)(ii) and so is labelled as such in the examination

Requests by Centre 22151 31/03/2003

==

Date Requested	Candidate Number	Subject Ref Code	Original Mark	Original Mark	Remark Mark	New Grade
26/03/2003	1001	54821	70	D	73	D
26/03/2003	1234	01325	58	D	55	D
26/03/2003	1234	20094	35	E	32	E
26/03/2003	1234	28181	40	U		
26/03/2003	1234	54821	50	U	49	U
26/03/2003	4455	54821	76	C	80	B
26/03/2003	4567	01325	66	C	59	D
26/03/2003	5678	01325	99	A	100	A
26/03/2003	6789	01325	0	U	0	U
26/03/2003	6789	54821	63	E		
26/03/2003	7456	54821	72	D		

Today's Remarks resulting in Grade Changes 31/03/2003

==

Date Requested	Centre Number	Candidate Number	Subject Ref Code	Orig. Mark	Orig. Grade	Remark Mark	New Grade	
26/03/2003	12345	4556	54821	84	B	85	A	
26/03/2003	12345	7799	01325	47	U	51	E	
26/03/2003	22151	4455	54821	76	C	80	B	
26/03/2003	22151	4567	01325	66	C	59	D	*Q4 (c) (ii)*
26/03/2003	23456	2222	54821	84	B	85	A	

Q2 (a) (ii)

```
Requests outstanding after 3 weeks as on 01/05/2003
======================================================
```

Date Requested	Centre Number	Candidate Number	Subject Ref Code	Original Mark	Original Grade
26/03/2003	22151	1234	28181	40	U
26/03/2003	22151	6789	54821	63	E
26/03/2003	22151	7456	54821	72	D
26/03/2003	77777	0100	28181	65	D
26/03/2003	77777	1234	54821	47	U
26/03/2003	80000	3456	28181	50	E
26/03/2003	10000	3456	54821	19	U

United Kingdom Awarding Body

Centre Number : 22151

31/03/2003

Result of remark request
========================

Candidate Number	Candidate Name	Subject Ref Code	Original Mark	Original Grade
6789	Anna Karenina	01325	0	U

No change to marks or grade

Q3 (a) (i)

Q3 (b)

United Kingdom Awarding Body

Centre Number : 22151

31/03/2003

Result of remark request
=========================

Candidate Number	Candidate Name		Subject Ref Code	Original Mark	Original Grade
1001		Oliver Twist	54821	70	D

The revised number of marks is   73.
No change of grade   Q4 (c) (i)

United Kingdom Awarding Body

Centre Number : 22151

31/03/2003

Result of remark request
========================

Candidate Number	Candidate Name	Subject Ref Code	Original Mark	Original Grade
4455	Chris Evans	54821	76	C

The revised number of marks is 80.
Revised grade: B

United Kingdom Awarding Body

System Documentation

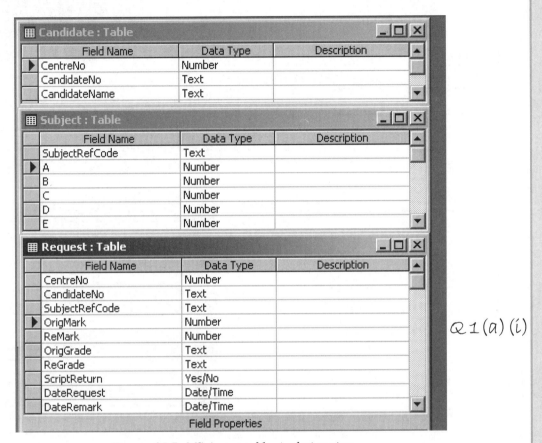

Candidate : Table

Field Name	Data Type	Description
CentreNo	Number	
CandidateNo	Text	
CandidateName	Text	

Subject : Table

Field Name	Data Type	Description
SubjectRefCode	Text	
A	Number	
B	Number	
C	Number	
D	Number	
E	Number	

Request : Table

Field Name	Data Type	Description
CentreNo	Number	
CandidateNo	Text	
SubjectRefCode	Text	
OrigMark	Number	
ReMark	Number	
OrigGrade	Text	
ReGrade	Text	
ScriptReturn	Yes/No	
DateRequest	Date/Time	
DateRemark	Date/Time	

Field Properties

Q1(a)(i)

Figure: 25.7: MS Access tables in design view

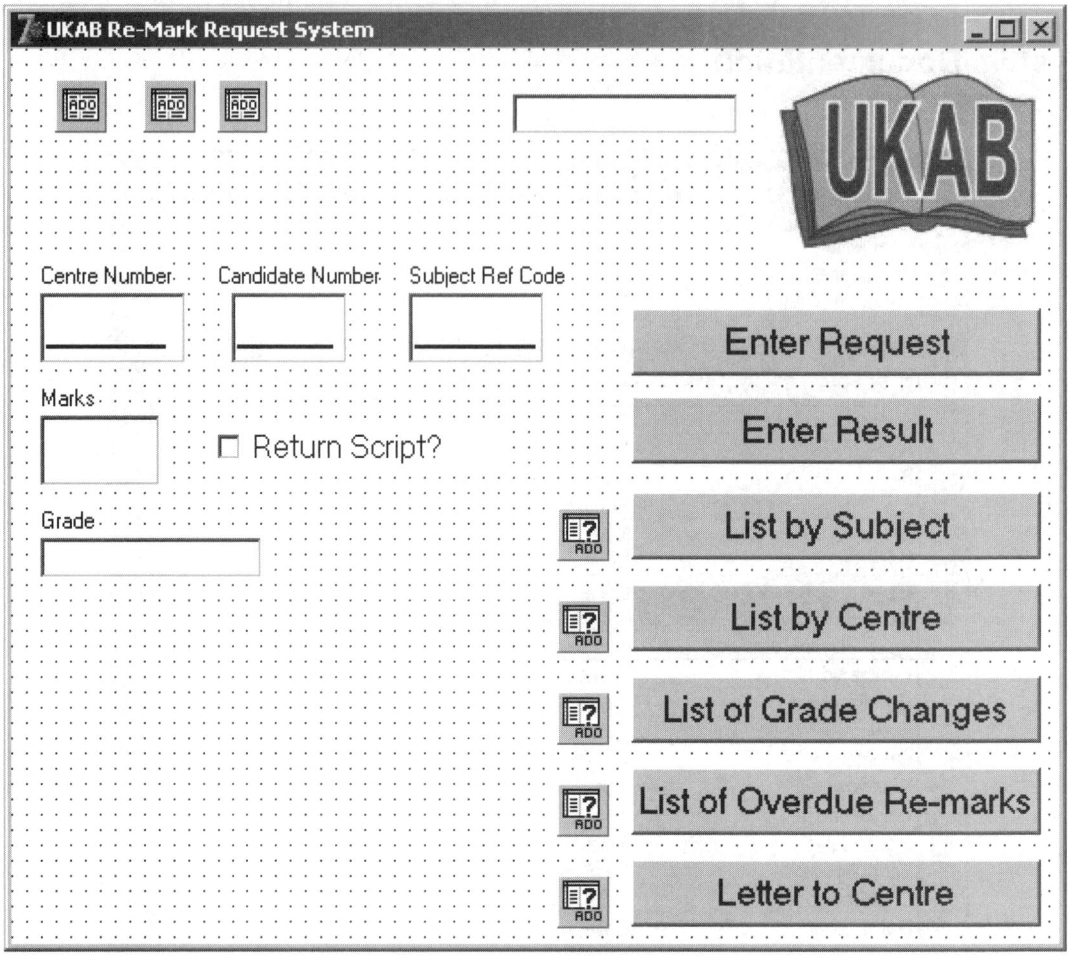

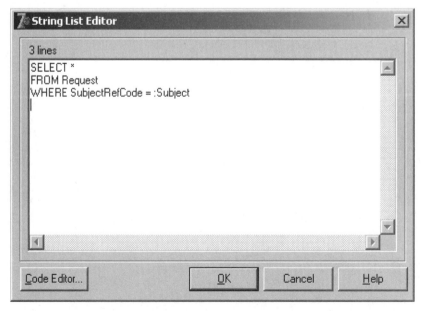

Figure 25.8: User Interface in design view

Figure 25.9: SQL statement for adoqListBySubject

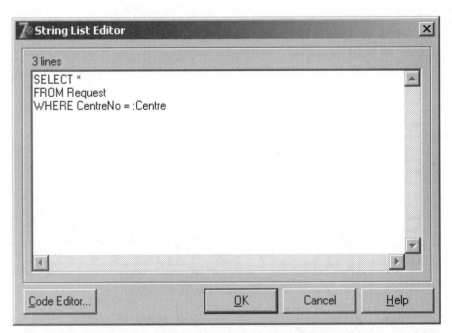

Figure 25.10: SQL statement for adoqListByCentre

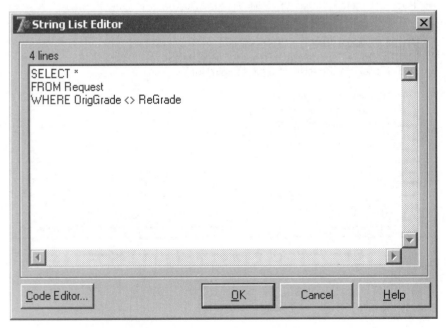

Figure 25.11: SQL statement for adoqListChanges

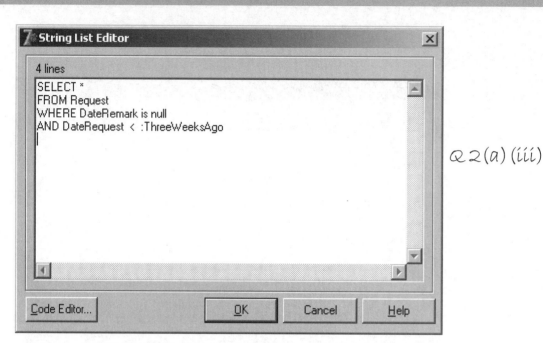

Q2(a)(iii)

Figure 25.12: SQL statement for adoqOverdue

Note: *This SQL statement was copied from the SQL generated by Access by performing a QBE*

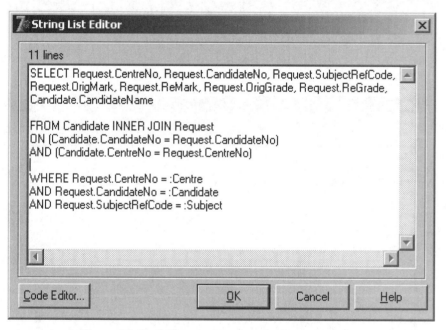

Figure 25.13: SQL statement for adoqLetterToCentre

```
unit Unit1;

interface

uses
  Windows, Messages, SysUtils, Variants, Classes, Graphics, Controls,
  Forms, Dialogs, Grids, DBGrids, DB, ADODB, jpeg, ExtCtrls, DBCtrls,
  StdCtrls, Mask;

type
  TfrmUKAB = class(TForm)
    adotSubjects: TADOTable;
    adotRequests: TADOTable;
    Image1: TImage;
    adotCandidate: TADOTable;
    EnterRequest: TButton;
    medtCandidateNo: TMaskEdit;
    Label1: TLabel;
    medtCentreNo: TMaskEdit;
    Label2: TLabel;
    medtSubjectRefCode: TMaskEdit;
    Label3: TLabel;
    chkReturnScript: TCheckBox;
    Label4: TLabel;
    btnEnterResult: TButton;
    edtMark: TEdit;
    ledtGrade: TLabeledEdit;
    adoqListBySubject: TADOQuery;
    btnListBySubject: TButton;
    btnListByCentre: TButton;
    btnGradeChanges: TButton;
    btnOverdue: TButton;
    btnLetterToCentre: TButton;
    adoqListByCentre: TADOQuery;
    adoqListChanges: TADOQuery;
    adoqOverdue: TADOQuery;
    adoqLetterToCentre: TADOQuery;
    procedure EnterRequestClick(Sender: TObject);
    procedure btnEnterResultClick(Sender: TObject);
    procedure btnListBySubjectClick(Sender: TObject);
    procedure btnListByCentreClick(Sender: TObject);
    procedure btnGradeChangesClick(Sender: TObject);
    procedure btnOverdueClick(Sender: TObject);
    procedure btnLetterToCentreClick(Sender: TObject);
  private
    { Private declarations }
  public
    { Public declarations }
  end;
```

```
var
  frmUKAB: TfrmUKAB;

implementation

{$R *.dfm}

uses Printers;

var Output : TextFile;

function ValidCentreNo : Boolean;
var CentreNo : Integer;
begin
  if  not (frmUKAB.medtCentreNo.Text = '        ')
    then       // digits entered
      begin
        CentreNo := StrToInt(frmUKAB.medtCentreNo.Text);
        if (CentreNo <10000) or (CentreNo > 80000)
          then
            begin
              ShowMessage ('Centre Number out of range');
              frmUKAB.medtCentreNo.SetFocus; Result := False;
            end
          else Result := True;
      end
    else          // no digits entered
      begin
        ShowMessage ('Please enter Centre Number');
        frmUKAB.medtCentreNo.SetFocus;  Result := False;
      end;
end;


function ValidCandidateNo : Boolean;
begin
  if  not (frmUKAB.medtCandidateNo.Text = '       ')
    then               // digits entered
      Result := True
    else               // no digits entered
      begin
        ShowMessage ('Please enter Candidate Number');
        frmUKAB.medtCandidateNo.SetFocus;
        Result := False;
      end;
end;
```

```
function ValidSubjectRefCode : Boolean;
begin
  if frmUKAB.adotSubjects.Locate('SubjectRefCode',
      frmUKAB.medtSubjectRefCode.text,[])
    then                  // valid subject ref code entered
      Result := True
    else                  // not a valid subject ref code
      begin
        ShowMessage ('Please enter valid Subject Ref Code');
        frmUKAB.medtSubjectRefCode.SetFocus;
        Result := False;
      end;
end;


function ValidMark : Boolean;
var Mark : Integer;
begin
  try
    Mark := StrToInt (frmUKAB.edtMark.Text);
     if (Mark >= 0) and (Mark <=100)
        then Result := True
        else    // number not within range
          begin
            ShowMessage ('Please enter marks within range');
            frmUKAB.edtMark.SetFocus;
            Result := False;
          end;
  except
    ShowMessage ('Please enter marks');
    frmUKAB.edtMark.SetFocus; Result := False;
  end; {except}
end;


function ValidRequest : Boolean;
begin
  if not frmUKAB.adotRequests.Locate('CentreNo; CandidateNo;
      SubjectRefCode', VarArrayOf([frmUKAB.medtCentreNo.Text,
      frmUKAB.medtCandidateNo.Text,
      frmUKAB.medtSubjectRefCode.Text]),[])
    then
      Result := True
    else
      begin
        Result := False;
        ShowMessage ('This is not a unique request')
      end;
end;
```

```
procedure FindGrade;
var Mark : Byte; Grade: Char;
begin
  Mark := StrToInt(frmUKAB.edtMark.Text);
  Grade := 'A';
  while  (Mark < frmUKAB.adotSubjects[Grade]) and (Grade < 'E')
    do  Grade := Succ(Grade);    //get next letter grade
  if (Mark < frmUKAB.adotSubjects[Grade])
    then frmUKAB.ledtGrade.Text := 'U'
    else frmUKAB.ledtGrade.Text := Grade;
end;


procedure InitialisePrinter;
begin
  AssignPrn (Output);
  Rewrite (Output);
  Printer.Canvas.Font.Name := 'Courier New';
  Printer.Canvas.Font.Size := 14;
end;


procedure TfrmUKAB.btnEnterResultClick(Sender: TObject);
begin
    if  ValidCentreNo and ValidCandidateNo and ValidSubjectRefCode
      then
        if ValidMark
          then
            begin
              FindGrade;
              if not adotRequests.Locate('CentreNo; CandidateNo;
                      SubjectRefCode',
                VarArrayOf ([medtCentreNo.Text,medtCandidateNo.Text,
                medtSubjectRefCode.Text]),[])
                then ShowMessage ('Not a valid request')
                else
                  begin
                    adotRequests.Edit;
                    adotRequests['ReMark'] := edtMark.Text;
                    adotRequests['ReGrade'] := ledtGrade.Text;
                    adotRequests['DateRemark'] := Date;
                    adotRequests.Post;
                  end;
            end;
end;
```

```
procedure TfrmUKAB.EnterRequestClick(Sender: TObject);
var Name: String;
begin
  if  ValidCentreNo and ValidCandidateNo and ValidSubjectRefCode
    then
      begin
        if not adotCandidate.Locate('CentreNo; CandidateNo',
             VarArrayOf ([medtCentreNo.Text,medtCandidateNo.Text]),[])
          then
            begin  // new candidate
              repeat
                Name := InputBox('New candidate',
                              'Please enter candidate''s full name','');
              until Name > '';
              adotCandidate.Append;
              adotCandidate['CentreNo'] := medtCentreNo.Text;
              adotCandidate['CandidateNo'] := medtCandidateNo.Text;
              adotCandidate['CandidateName'] := Name;
              adotCandidate.Post
            end;
        if ValidMark
          then
            begin
              FindGrade;
              if ValidRequest
                then
                  begin
                    adotRequests.Append;
                    adotRequests['CentreNo'] := medtCentreNo.Text;
                    adotRequests['CandidateNo'] := medtCandidateNo.Text;
                    adotRequests['SubjectRefCode'] :=
                                        medtSubjectRefCode.Text;
                    adotRequests['OrigMark'] := edtMark.Text;
                    adotRequests['OrigGrade'] := ledtGrade.Text;
                    adotRequests['ScriptReturn'] :=
                                        chkReturnScript.Checked;
                    adotRequests['DateRequest'] := Date;
                    adotRequests.Post;
                    medtCentreNo.Text := '';
                    medtCandidateNo.Text := '';
                    medtSubjectRefCode.Text := '';
                    edtMark.Text := '';
                    ledtGrade.Text := '';
                    chkReturnScript.Checked := False;
                  end;
            end;
      end;
end;
```

Q 4 (b)

```
procedure TfrmUKAB.btnListBySubjectClick(Sender: TObject);
begin
  adoqListBySubject.Close;
  adoqListBySubject.Parameters[0].Value := medtSubjectRefCode.Text;   Q 2(a)(i)
  adoqListBySubject.Open;
  adoqListBySubject.First;
  InitialisePrinter;
  Printer.Canvas.Font.Style := [fsBold];
  Write (Output, '  Requests by Subject Ref Code ',
                      medtSubjectRefCode.Text, '  ');
  Writeln (Output, DateToStr(Date));
  Writeln (Output, '  ===============================================');
  Writeln (Output);
  Printer.Canvas.Font.Style := [];
  Write (Output, 'Date':6, 'Centre':14, 'Candidate':11, 'Original':10);
  Writeln (Output, 'Original':10, 'Remark':8, 'New':5);
  Write (Output, 'Requested':11, 'Number':9, 'Number':8);
  Writeln (Output, 'Mark':9, 'Grade':11, 'Mark':9, 'Grade':9);
  while not adoqListBySubject.Eof
    do
      begin
        Write (Output, adoqListBySubject['DateRequest']:12);
        Write (Output, adoqListBySubject['CentreNo']:7);
        Write (Output, adoqListBySubject['CandidateNo']:7);
        Write (Output, adoqListBySubject['OrigMark']:9);
        Write (Output, adoqListBySubject['OrigGrade']:9);
        if  adoqListBySubject['DateReMark'] > 0
          then
            begin
              Write (Output, adoqListBySubject['ReMark']:11);
              Writeln (Output, adoqListBySubject['ReGrade']:7);
            end
          else Writeln(Output);
          adoqListBySubject.Next;
      end;
  CloseFile (Output);
end;


procedure TfrmUKAB.btnListByCentreClick(Sender: TObject);
begin
  adoqListByCentre.Close;
  adoqListByCentre.Parameters[0].Value := medtCentreNo.Text;
  adoqListByCentre.Open;
  adoqListByCentre.First;

  InitialisePrinter;
  Printer.Canvas.Font.Style := [fsBold];
  Write (Output, '  Requests by Centre ', medtCentreNo.Text, '   ');
  Writeln (Output, DateToStr(Date));
```

```
Writeln (Output, '  ======================================');
Writeln (Output);
Printer.Canvas.Font.Style := [];
Write (Output, 'Date':6, 'Candidate':16, 'Subject':9);
Writeln (Output, 'Original':11, 'Original':10, 'Remark':7, 'New':5);
Write (Output, 'Requested':11, 'Number':8,'Ref Code':13);
Writeln (Output, 'Mark':6, 'Grade':11, 'Mark':8, 'Grade':9);
while not adoqListByCentre.Eof
  do
    begin
       Write (Output, adoqListByCentre['DateRequest']:12);
       Write (Output, adoqListByCentre['CandidateNo']:5);
       Write (Output, adoqListByCentre['SubjectRefCode']:12);
       Write (Output, adoqListByCentre['OrigMark']:7);
       Write (Output, adoqListByCentre['OrigGrade']:10);
       if  adoqListByCentre['DateRemark'] > 0
         then
           begin
             Write (Output, adoqListByCentre['ReMark']:9);
             Writeln (Output, adoqListByCentre['ReGrade']:7);
           end
         else Writeln(Output);
       adoqListByCentre.Next;
    end;
  CloseFile (Output)
end;
```

```
procedure TfrmUKAB.btnGradeChangesClick(Sender: TObject);
begin
  adoqListChanges.Close;
  adoqListChanges.Open;
  adoqListChanges.First;

  InitialisePrinter;
  Printer.Canvas.Font.Style := [fsBold];
  Write (Output, '  Today''s Remarks resulting in Grade Changes ');
  Writeln (Output, DateToStr(Date));
  Writeln (Output, '
=====================================================');
  Writeln (Output);
  Printer.Canvas.Font.Style := [];
  Write (Output, 'Date':6, 'Centre':13, 'Candidate':11);
  Write (Output, 'Subject':9, 'Orig.':7, 'Orig.':6);
  Writeln (Output, 'Remark':8, 'New':4);
  Write (Output, 'Requested':11, 'Number':8, 'Number':8);
  Write (Output,'Ref Code':13, 'Mark':5, 'Grade':7);
  Writeln (Output, 'Mark':6, 'Grade':7);
  while not adoqListChanges.Eof
    do
      begin
        Write (Output, adoqListChanges['DateRequest']:12);
        Write (Output, adoqListChanges['CentreNo']:7);
        Write (Output, adoqListChanges['CandidateNo']:6);
        Write (Output, adoqListChanges['SubjectRefCode']:12);
        Write (Output, adoqListChanges['OrigMark']:6);
        Write (Output, adoqListChanges['OrigGrade']:5);
        Write (Output, adoqListChanges['ReMark']:8);
        Writeln (Output, adoqListChanges['ReGrade']:6);
        adoqListChanges.Next;
      end;
  CloseFile (Output);
end;
```

```
procedure TfrmUKAB.btnOverdueClick(Sender: TObject);
begin
  adoqOverdue.Close;
  adoqOverdue.Parameters[0].Value := DateToStr(StrToDate(edtDate.Text)-21);
  adoqOverdue.Open;
  adoqOverdue.First;

  InitialisePrinter;
  Printer.Canvas.Font.Style := [fsBold];
  Write (Output, '  Requests outstanding after 3 weeks as on ');
  Writeln (Output, DateToStr(Date));
  Writeln (Output, '  =================================================');
  Writeln (Output);
  Printer.Canvas.Font.Style := [];
  Write (Output, 'Date':6, 'Centre':14, 'Candidate':11);
  Writeln (Output, 'Subject':9, 'Original':11, 'Original':11);
  Write (Output, 'Requested':11, 'Number':9, 'Number':8);
  Writeln (Output, 'Ref Code':13, 'Mark':6, 'Grade':12);
  while not adoqOverdue.Eof
    do
      begin
        Write (Output,adoqOverdue['DateRequest']:12);
        Write (Output,adoqOverdue['CentreNo']:7);
        Write (Output,adoqOverdue['CandidateNo']:7);
        Write (Output,adoqOverdue['SubjectRefCode']:12);
        Write (Output,adoqOverdue['OrigMark']:7);
        Writeln (Output, adoqOverdue['OrigGrade']:10);
        adoqOverdue.Next;
      end;
  CloseFile (Output);
end;


procedure TfrmUKAB.FormCreate(Sender: TObject);
begin
  edtDate.Text := DateToStr(Date);  // Display today's date
end;
```

Q2(a)(iii)

```
procedure TfrmUKAB.btnLetterToCentreClick(Sender: TObject);
var Count : Integer;
begin
  adoqLetterToCentre.Close;
  adoqLetterToCentre.Parameters[0].Value := medtCentreNo.Text;
  adoqLetterToCentre.Parameters[1].Value := medtCandidateNo.Text;
  adoqLetterToCentre.Parameters[2].Value := medtSubjectRefCode.Text;
  adoqLetterToCentre.Open;
  adoqLetterToCentre.First;
  InitialisePrinter;
  Printer.Canvas.Font.Style := [fsBold];
  for Count := 1 to 15   {empty lines for letterhead}
    do Writeln (Output);
  Write (Output, '  Centre Number : ');
  Writeln (Output, medtCentreNo.Text);
  Writeln (Output, DateToStr(Date):60);
  Writeln (Output, '  Result of remark request');
  Writeln (Output, '  =======================');
  Writeln (Output);
  Printer.Canvas.Font.Style := [];
  Write (Output, 'Candidate':11, 'Candidate':11, 'Subject':21);
  Writeln (Output, 'Original':11, 'Original':10);
  Write (Output, 'Number':8, 'Name':9, 'Ref Code':27);
  Writeln (Output, 'Mark':6, 'Grade':11);
  Write (Output,adoqLetterToCentre['CandidateNo']:6,'        ');
  Write (Output,adoqLetterToCentre['CandidateName']:21);
  Write (Output,adoqLetterToCentre['SubjectRefCode']:7);
  Write (Output, adoqLetterToCentre['OrigMark']:7);
  Writeln (Output, adoqLetterToCentre['OrigGrade']:9);
  Writeln (Output);
  if   adoqLetterToCentre['ReMark'] <> adoqLetterToCentre['OrigMark']
    then
      begin
        Write (Output, '  The revised number of marks is ');
        Writeln (Output, adoqLetterToCentre['ReMark']:4,'.');
        if adoqLetterToCentre['OrigGrade'] <>
             adoqLetterToCentre['ReGrade']
          then
            begin
              Write (Output, '  Revised grade: ');
              Writeln (Output, adoqLetterToCentre['ReGrade']:2);
            end
          else
            Writeln (Output, '  No change of grade.');
      end
    else Writeln(Output, '  No change to marks or grade');
  CloseFile (Output);
end;
end.
```

Selected questions with answers from the AQA May 2003 Examination paper for Unit 3 (CPT3)

Question 2

This question relates to the IMPLEMENTATION process.
(a) In order to produce the requested hard copy lists, your solution has to find certain records. Exactly how did your solution find:

(i) records where re-marks have been requested for a particular subject;

> The program searches through all requests held, and compares the subject code with the Subject Reference Code for the particular subject.

(2 marks)

Where in your documentation is your coding to find this data?

Page number   D-30

(1 mark)

(Write Q2(a)(i) in the margin, in the correct place, on that page.)

(ii) records where the candidate's mark has changed causing a change in grade;

> The record storing the request details has fields for both the original grade and the re-mark grade. An SQL statement is called which selects the appropriate records.

(2 marks)

Where is a hard copy of such a list in your documentation?
Page number   D-15

(1 mark)

(Write Q2(a)(ii) in the margin, in the correct place, on that page.)

(iii) records where re-marks have not been completed in the required three-week period?

> I stored the date on which the re-mark was done, so I can check where this date is not filled in and the date the request was received is more than 21 days from 'today'.

(3 marks)

Give the page number either of the coding to produce this list or a hard copy of this list in your documentation.

Page number   D-24 for SQL, page D-33 for program call *(1 mark)*

(Write Q 2(a)(iii) in the margin, in the correct place, on that page.)

(b) You were asked to produce a daily list of those re-marks where the candidate's grade has been affected by a mark change. UKAB decides it also needs a daily list of those re-marks where the grade has not changed, whether or not the mark had been changed.

Write an algorithm to produce this list.

```
For each request do
    If re-mark date = today's date
        AND original grade = re-mark grade
        Then print out re-mark details
    Endif
End loop
```

(5 marks)

Total marks 15

Question 3

This question relates to the REPORT DESIGN process.

(a) (i) On which page of your documentation is a hard copy of the document to be returned to centres, complete with UKAB logo?

Page number   D-17   *(1 mark)*

(Write Q3(a)(i) in the margin, in the correct place, on that page.)

(ii) How did you input the logo and position it on this document?

I scanned in the logo from the specification and placed it in an empty word-processed document and printed it to make pre-printed stationery. I had to make sure when printing the document that I left enough empty lines not to print over the letterhead.   *(3 marks)*

(b) Give two criteria that you have considered for the design of this document, other than using the logo, and say how you have used each of them.

1 Easy to read information – used bold type for centre details, underlined purpose of document.

2 Layout easy to follow – heading carefully lined up over the data.   *(4 marks)*

(Write Q 3(b) in the margin of your document, in the correct place(s) on the page(s), where these two aspects of design are demonstrated.)

(2 marks)
Total marks 10

Question 4

This question relates to the TESTING and VALIDATION process.

(a) How did your solution prevent the entry of a mark greater than 100?

When the program asks for the original mark it will only move to the next question if a number between 0 and 100 is typed in.

(1 mark)

(b) How did you ensure that your solution would allow two candidates with the same candidate number but from different centres?

I used test data of two candidates with the same number from different centres doing the same subject. So the candidate numbers and subject reference codes were the same but the centre numbers were different.

(2 marks)

Where is this made clear in your documentation?
Page number   D-29

(1 mark)

(Write Q4(b) in the margin, in the correct place, on that page.)

(c) What test data did you use for a candidate's mark being
(i) increased;   *original mark 70, new mark 73*
(ii) decreased?   *original mark 66, new mark 59*

(2 marks)

Where is the evidence of this testing in your documentation?

Page number   D-18   And   D-15   *(2 marks)*

(Write Q 4(c)(i) and 4 (c)(ii) in the margin, in the correct places, on those pages.)

Total marks 8

Appendix A

Using the Debugger

No matter how careful you are when writing code, your programs are likely to contain errors, or *bugs*, that prevent them from running the way you intended.

There are three basic types of program errors:

o Syntax errors

o Logic errors

o Runtime errors

The compiler will find your syntax errors and display them in the Compiler Message window. (See Figure 1.6 and Figure 12.8.)

Debugging is the process of locating and fixing runtime errors and logic errors in your programs. The Delphi integrated debugger enables you to:

o Control the execution of your program

o Monitor the values of variables and items in data structures

o Modify the values of data items while debugging

By running to specific program locations and viewing the state of your program at those places, you can monitor how your program behaves and find the areas where it is not behaving as you intended.

If you receive messages (such as error or status messages) while debugging an application, you can type *Ctrl+C* in the message box to copy the text of the message to the clipboard.

If you want to use the debugger you must ensure it is switched on before you compile and run your program.

- Turn on the debugger: Select **Tools, Debugger Options, General**.
- Check the **Integrated Debugger** option and click on **OK**.

This will allow you to step through your program, using **Run, Trace Into**.

- After each click of the **Trace Into** button (or **F7**) hover the mouse over the variable names in your program: the current value of the variable pointed to will pop up.

You can make this inspection of variable values easier by adding a watch window:

- Select **Run, Add Watch ...** and you will see the following window:

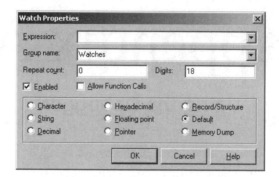

Figure A.1: Adding a watch

- Type one of your variable names into the **Expression** box and click **OK**. You can add as many variable names as you want to know the value of during your trace.

- Trace into your program and watch the values change as the program is executed with each pressing of **F7** (the *Trace Into* shortcut).

You may find your watch window displays **Variable inaccessible here due to optimisation**. You can switch optimisation off so as to see the state of your variable values better:

- Add the compiler directive {$OPTIMIZATION OFF} before the **uses** clause.

In fact you can add this line anywhere you want to switch optimisation off, and switch it back on later with {$OPTIMIZATION ON}

If you do not want to trace through the whole of your program you can add breakpoints at the places where you want to trace through the execution one instruction at a time.

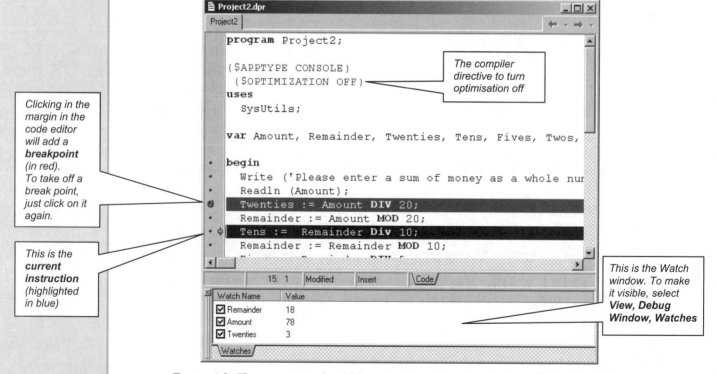

Figure A.2: The program code with breakpoint, current instruction and Watch window

Appendix B

Common Errors and Possible Solutions

Pascal

Problem:	Program statements do not seem to be recognised
Possible Reason:	Incorrect use of comment brackets or string delimiters
Solution:	Choose a code format that allows you to see easily what are comments and what are strings. Right-click in the **Code Editor** window and choose **Properties** from the pop-up menu. Choose the **Display** tab for choosing Font and Font Size and the **Color** tab for customising your program code format. For example choose red for strings and blue for comments: 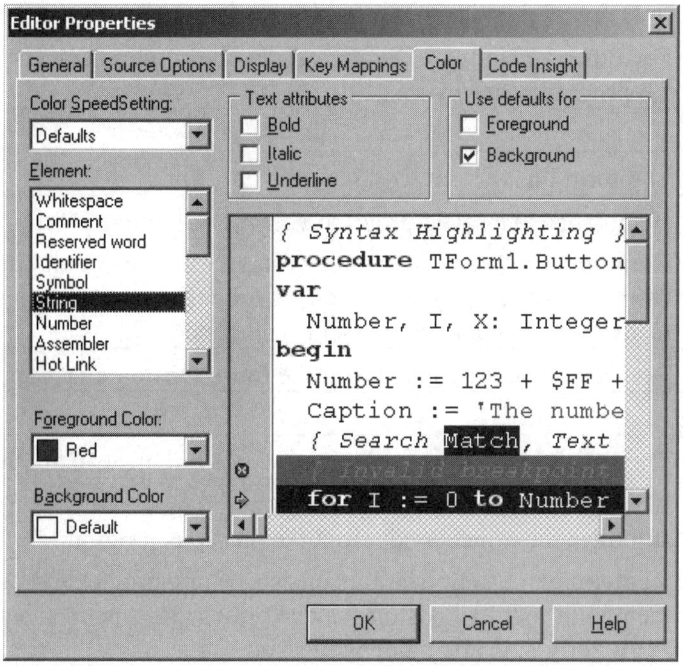

Figure B.1: Editor Properties, Color tab

Problem:	Program compiles but won't run. Error message 'Exception EinOutError....'
Possible Reason:	Deleted compiler directive.
Solution:	Retype the line {$APPTYPE CONSOLE} after the program header.

Problem:	Program compiles but loops do not seem to be executed
Possible reason:	Semicolon immediately after the keyword do
Solution:	Delete semicolon after do. Semicolon should come only after the statement to be repeated.

Problem:	Compilation error 'Identifier redeclared....', but I have not used any variable name twice.
Possible Reason:	Program was saved with the same name as one of the variables or other identifiers.
Solution:	Resave your program under a unique identifier name (using **Save As**).

Problem:	My program crashes but I don't understand the debugger message.
Solution:	Switch off the integrated debugger by choosing **Tools, Debugger Options, General** and uncheck the **Integrated Debugger** option at the bottom of the window.

Delphi

Problem:	I changed some properties of components accidentally, but cannot remember which.
Solution:	In Delphi 7 properties that have been changed from the default are shown in bold. For other versions of Delphi, get another component of the same type and compare the properties one by one.

Problem:	The form I have been working on won't run.
Possible Reason:	If you opened a saved program you opened only the form, not the project. **Remember:** An application consists of one project and one or more forms, each with their unit code. Choosing **New Application** opens a new project and a new form, ready for you to add components and code.
Solution:	Save any changes you made to the form. Open the project rather than the form.

Problem:	The form I have been working on won't run, instead another form is visible.
Possible Reason:	If it is a new form created after completing a previous application, you are likely to still have the project open from the previous program. **Remember:** An application consists of one project and one or more forms, each with their unit code. Choosing **New Application** opens a new project and a new form, ready for you to add components and code.
Solution:	Save the project under a different name, using **File, Save Project As** (to keep the original for the previous program). Then add the new form to the project, using **Project, Add to Project** and then choose the name of the new form from the explorer window. Next remove the unwanted form from the project, using **Project, Remove from Project** and choose the unwanted form from the explorer window. **Save All**! If it still won't show the correct form when you try and run the application, select **Project, Options …** and select the correct form from the drop-down list of **Main form**.

Problem:	My program crashes but I don't understand the debugger message.
Solution:	Switch off the integrated debugger by choosing **Tools, Debugger Options, General** and uncheck the **Integrated debugging** option at the bottom of the window.

Problem:	I get the compiler message 'Unsatisfied forward or external declaration:' with the name of an event handler and the event-handler name in the interface section of the program code is highlighted.
Possible Reason:	You deleted the event-handler because you didn't need it any more.
Solution:	In future only remove the code between `begin` and `end` of any event-handler you no longer want (i.e. only the code you wrote). Delphi will clear up the rest. Retype the header of the event handler followed by `begin  end;` If you are not sure of the format, look at another event-handler. Next time you compile the code, Delphi will tidy up any unwanted event-handlers.

Problem:	I get the compiler message 'Undeclared identifier:' with the name of an event-handler.
Possible Reason:	You wrote the event-handler header yourself rather than let Delphi provide the template for you.
Solution:	Double-click on the component (or on its appropriate event in the object inspector) for which you wrote the event-handler and cut and paste the code into the template provided.

Problem:	The compiler gives me the message 'Program or Unit ... recursively uses itself.' *Figure B.2: Compiler message*
Reason:	You have saved your form and code under the same identifier as one of the units in the units clause (in the example above *Messages*).

Solution:	Resave your form (and unit) under another name using **Save As**.
	Then you need to delete the unit with the duplicate name from the folder in which you have saved your project.
	Make sure you choose names that are unique. Check what units are listed in the **uses** clause.
	Remember: the form and its corresponding unit are saved under the same name (with different extensions). The project and its resource files are saved under a different name. Try and choose sensible names. You may wish to reuse a form and its unit in another project. The project name is also used for the compiled code (the *.exe* file).

Delphi and MS Access

Problem:	Trying to open an application that is linked to a database gives this error:
	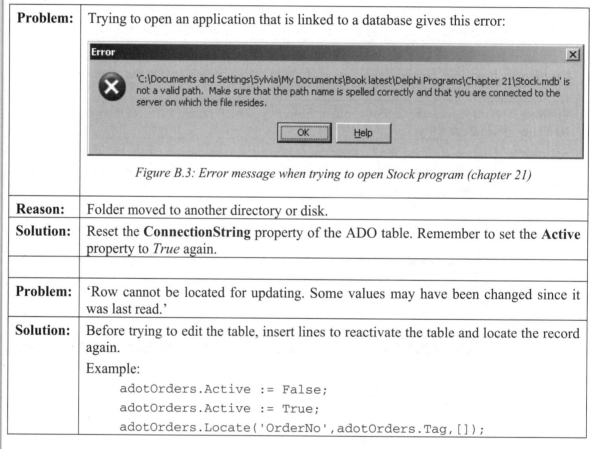
	Figure B.3: Error message when trying to open Stock program (chapter 21)
Reason:	Folder moved to another directory or disk.
Solution:	Reset the **ConnectionString** property of the ADO table. Remember to set the **Active** property to *True* again.
Problem:	'Row cannot be located for updating. Some values may have been changed since it was last read.'
Solution:	Before trying to edit the table, insert lines to reactivate the table and locate the record again.
	Example:

	<pre>adotOrders.Active := False;
	adotOrders.Active := True;
	adotOrders.Locate('OrderNo',adotOrders.Tag,[]);</pre>

Appendix C

Standard Functions and Procedures

The table below lists frequently used procedures and functions found in Borland product libraries. This is not an exhaustive inventory of standard routines.

To find out what parameters these routines require, look in Delphi Help.

Procedure/Function	Description
ArcTan	Calculates the arctangent of the given number.
Beep	Generates a standard beep.
Break	Causes control to exit a for, while, or repeat statement.
ByteToCharIndex	Returns the position of the character containing a specified byte in a string.
Chr	Returns the character for a specified integer value.
Close	Closes the application.
CompareMem	Performs a binary comparison of two memory images.
CompareStr	Compares strings case sensitively.
CompareText	Compares strings by ordinal value and is not case sensitive.
Concat	Concatenates an arbitrary number of strings
Continue	Returns control to the next iteration of for, while, or repeat statements.
Copy	Returns a substring of a string or a segment of a dynamic array.
Cos	Calculates the cosine of an angle.
CurrToStr	Converts a currency variable to a string.
Date	Returns the current date.
DateTimeToStr	Converts a variable of type TDateTime to a string.
DateToStr	Converts a variable of type TDateTime to a string.
Dec	Decrements an ordinal variable or a typed pointer variable.
Delete	Removes a substring of *Count* characters from string *S* starting with *S[Index]*.
Exit	Exits from the current procedure.
Exp	Calculates the exponential of *X*.
FillChar	Fills contiguous bytes with a specified value.
FloatToStr	Converts a floating point value to a string.
FloatToStrF	Converts a floating point value to a string, using specified format.

FmtLoadStr	Returns formatted output using a resourced format string.
FmtStr	Assembles a formatted string from a series of arrays.
Format	Assembles a string from a format string and a series of arrays.
FormatDateTime	Formats a date-and-time value.
FormatFloat	Formats a floating point value.
Halt	Initiates abnormal termination of a program.
High	Returns the highest value in the range of a type, array, or string.
Inc	Increments an ordinal variable or a typed pointer variable.
InputBox	Displays an input dialog box that lets the user enter a string, double, or integer.
Insert	Inserts a substring at a specified point in a string.
Int	Returns the integer part of a real number.
IntToStr	Converts an integer to a string.
LeftStr	Returns the leading characters of *String* up to a length of *Count* characters.
Length	Returns the length of a string or array.
Low	Returns the lowest value in the range of a type, array, or string.
LowerCase	Converts an ASCII string to lowercase.
Max	Returns the greater value of two.
MaxIntValue	Returns the largest signed value in an integer array.
MaxValue	Returns the largest signed value in an array.
MessageDlg	Brings up a message box (choice of formats) and obtains the user's response (using a selection of buttons).
MidStr	Returns a substring *Count* characters at *String*[*Start*].
Min	Returns the smaller value of two.
MinIntValue	Returns the smallest signed value in an integer array.
MinValue	Returns smallest signed value in an array.
Now	Returns the current date and time.
Odd	Returns true if *X* is an odd number, false if *X* is even.
Ord	Returns the ordinal integer value of an ordinal-type expression.
Pi	Returns 3.1415926535897932385.
Pos	Returns the index of the first single-byte character of a specified substring in a string.
Pred	Returns the predecessor of an ordinal value.
Random	Generates random numbers within a specified range.
Randomize	Initializes the built-in random number generator with a random value, obtained from the system clock.
RandomRange	Returns a random integer from the range that extends between *From* and *To* inclusive.

ReverseString	Returns the string specified with the characters in reverse order.
RightStr	Returns the trailing characters of *String* up to a length of *Count* characters.
Round	Returns the value of a real rounded to the nearest whole number.
ShowMessage	Displays a message box with an unformatted string and an OK button.
ShowMessageFmt	Displays a message box with a formatted string and an OK button.
Sign	Returns 1,0 or –1, depending on whether the value is positive, negative, or zero.
Sin	Returns the sine of an angle in radians.
SizeOf	Returns the number of bytes occupied by a variable or type.
Sqr	Returns the square of a number.
Sqrt	Returns the square root of a number.
Str	Converts an integer or real number into a string.
StrToCurr	Converts a string to a currency value.
StrToDate	Converts a string to a date format (TDateTime).
StrToDateTime	Converts a string to a TDateTime.
StrToFloat	Converts a string to a floating-point value.
StrToInt	Converts a string to an integer.
StrToTime	Converts a string to a time format (TDateTime).
StrUpper	Returns an ASCII string in upper case.
Succ	Returns the successor of an ordinal value.
Sum	Returns the sum of the elements from an array.
Time	Returns the current time.
TimeToStr	Converts a variable of type TDateTime to a string.
Trim	Removes leading and trailing spaces and control characters from the given string.
TrimLeft	Returns a copy of the string with leading spaces and control characters removed.
TrimRight	Returns a copy of the string with trailing spaces and control characters removed.
Trunc	Truncates a real number to an integer.
UpCase	Converts a character to uppercase.
UpperCase	Returns a string in uppercase.
Val	Converts a string to a numeric representation.

Input and Output routines for all files	
AssignFile	Assigns the name of an external file to a file variable.
ChDir	Changes the current directory.
CloseFile	Closes an open file.
Eof	Returns the end-of-file status of a file.
Eoln	Returns the end-of-line status of a text file.
Erase	Erases an external file.
GetDir	Returns the current directory of a specified drive.
IOResult	Returns an integer value that is the status of the last I/O function performed.
MkDir	Creates a subdirectory.
Read	Reads one or more values from a file into one or more variables.
Rename	Renames an external file.
Reset	Opens an existing file.
Rewrite	Creates and opens a new file.
RmDir	Removes an empty subdirectory.
Write	Writes one or more values to a file.
Input and output routines for text files only	
Append	Opens an existing text file for appending.
AssignPrn	Assigns a text file variable to the printer.
Flush	Flushes the buffer of an output text file.
Readln	Does what Read does and then skips to beginning of next line in the text file.
SeekEof	Returns the end-of-file status of a text file.
SeekEoln	Returns the end-of-line status of a text file.
SetTextBuf	Assigns an I/O buffer to a text file.
Writeln	Does the same as Write, and then writes an end-of-line marker to the text file.
Input and output routines for typed files only	
FilePos	Returns the current file position of a file.
FileSize	Returns the current size of a file.
Seek	Moves the current position of a file to a specified component.
Truncate	Truncates a file at the current file position.

Appendix D

Naming Convention for Delphi Components

Hungarian Notation

Dr Charles Simonyi[3] first introduced an identifier naming convention that adds a prefix in lower case to the capitalised identifier name to indicate the functional type of the identifier. This system became widely used in Microsoft Windows programming. Programmers using other environments have adopted variants of this notation. Below is a list of prefixes as recommended by Jeffrey McArthur[4].

Advantages of "Hungarian Notation" style naming convention:

o Programmers will be able to understand each others' code better

o Easier to invent new component identifiers

o The list of objects displayed in the object inspector is alphabetical. "Hungarian Notation" style naming forces objects of the same type to sort together

Recommended Prefixes for Delphi Components

Palette Page	Component	Prefix
Standard	TButton	btn
	TCheckBox	chk
	TComboBox	cbo
	TEdit	edt
	TGroupBox	grp
	TLabel	lbl
	TListBox	lbo
	TMainMenu	mmnu
	TMemo	mem
	TMenuItem	mnu
	TPanel	pnl
	TPopupMenu	pmnu
	TRadioButton	rbtn
	TRadioGroup	rgrp
	TScollBar	sbr

---

[3] MSDN / Library / Hungarian Notation
Article by Charles Simonyi and Martin Heller *in Byte, August 1991 Vol1 6 No 8*
[4] ATLIS white pages – Delphi Source Code Naming Conventions

Additional	TBevel	bvl
	TBitBtn	bbtn
	TCheckListBox	clbo
	TDrawGrid	dgrd
	TImage	img
	TLabeledEdit	ledt
	TLCDNumber	lcdn
	TMaskEdit	medt
	TScrollBox	sbo
	TShape	shp
	TSpeedButton	sbtn
	TStringGrid	sgrd
System	TDirectoryTreeView	dir
	TFileEdit	filedt
	TFileIconView	filicn
	TFilterComboBox	filt
	TMediaPlayer	mpl
	TOLEContainer	olec
	TPaintBox	pbx
	TTimer	tmr
Dialogs	TColorDialog	dlgcl
	TFindDialog	dlgfn
	TFontDialog	dlgft
	TOpenDialog	dlgop
	TPrintDialog	dlgpr
	TPrinterSetupDialog	dlgps
	TReplaceDialog	dlgrp
	TSaveDialog	dlgsv
Data Access	TDataSource	ds
Data Controls	TDBCheckBox	dbchk
	TDBComboBox	dbcbo
	TDBEdit	dbedt
	TDBGrid	dbgrd
	TDBimage	dbimg
	TDBListBox	dblbo
	TDBLookupComboBox	dblcbo
	TDBLookupListBox	dbllbo
	TDBMemo	dbmem
	TDBNavigator	dbnav
	TDBRadioGroup	dbrgrp
	TDBText	dbtxt
	TDBRichEdit	dbredt
	TDBCtrlGrid	dbcgrd
	TDBChart	dbch

Win32	TTabControl	tabc
	TPageControl	pgc
	TImageList	imgl
	TRichEdit	redt
	TTrackBar	trbar
	TProgressBar	pbar
	TUpDown	upd
	THotKey	hk
	TDateTimePicker	dtp
	TMonthCalendar	mc
	TTreeView	tv
	TListView	lv
	THeaderControl	hdrc
	TStatusBar	sbar
	TToolBar	tbar
	TPageScoller	pgscr
	TSpinEdit	sedt

Appendix E

Delphi Component Summary

Below is a summary of components, their properties, events and methods explored in the chapters of this book but there are many more properties, events and methods for you to explore. There are also many more components available within the Delphi environment as well as to download from the Internet. Try **www.delphiabout.com**

Component	Properties	Event	Method	Exercise
ADOTable	Name, ConnectionString, TableName, Active		Locate, First, Prior, Next, Last, Insert, Delete, Edit, Post, Cancel, Refresh, Append	Ch. 21
ADOQuery	Name, ConnectionString, SQL, Eof		Close, Open	Ch. 21
Button	Name, Caption, Alignment, Font	Click		Worked Example Ch.12
CheckBox	Name, Caption			Ex.13.4
ComboBox	Name, Text, Font, Items, ItemIndex Text	Change		Ex.13.1 Ex.18.3
DataSource	Name, DataSet			
DateTimePicker	Date			Ex.15.3
DBEdit	Name, ReadOnly, DataSource			Ch. 21
DBGrid	Name, DataSource, Columns Sub-properties: Width, Alignment, Title, Caption			Ch. 21
DBNavigator	Name, DataSource			Ch. 21
Edit	Name, Text Font.Color, Font.Style, Font.Size ReadOnly	Change	SetFocus	Ex.12.2 Ex.13.4 Ex.13.6 Ex.15.1 Ex.16.1

Component	Properties	Event	Method	Exercise
Form	Name, Caption			Worked Example Ch.12
			Show	Ex.20.1
	Visible		ShowModal	Ex.20.3
GroupBox	Name, Caption			Ex.13.4
Image	Name, Picture, Visible			Ex.12.1
	Top			Ex.14.7
Label	Name, Caption			Worked Example Ch.12
LabeledEdit	Name, Text, LabelPosition, EditLabel.Caption			Ex.12.3
ListBox	Name, Sorted		Clear, DeleteSelected, AddItem	Ex.12.3
	Font.Size, Height, Width, Columns			Ex.15.3
MaskEdit	Text, PasswordChar, EditMask			Ex.13.5
Memo	Name, Enabled, Text, Lines		Append	Ex.14.1
RadioGroup	Name, Caption, Items, ItemIndex			Ex.13.3
Shape	Name, Shape, Brush.Color,	Click		Ex.13.3
	Top, Height			Ex.15.5
SpinEdit	Name, Value,	Change		Ex.13.6
	MinValue, MaxValue			Ex. 14.1
StringGrid	ColCount, RowCount, DefaultColWidth, DefaultRowHeight			Ex.16.6
	Cells[ColIndex, RowIndex]			
Timer	Interval, Enabled	Timer		Ex.14.7

Appendix F

ASCII codes

Code	Char	Code	Char	Code	Char	Code	Char	Code	Char	Code	Char
1		46	.	91	[	136		181	µ	226	â
2		47	/	92	\	137		182	¶	227	ã
3		48	0	93	]	138		183	·	228	ä
4		49	1	94	^	139		184	¸	229	å
5		50	2	95	ˍ	140		185	¹	230	æ
6		51	3	96	`	141		186	º	231	ç
7	BEL	52	4	97	a	142		187	»	232	è
8		53	5	98	b	143		188	¼	233	é
9	TAB	54	6	99	c	144		189	½	234	ê
10	LF	55	7	100	d	145	´	190	¾	235	ë
11		56	8	101	e	146	´	191	¿	236	ì
12		57	9	102	f	147		192	À	237	í
13	CR	58	:	103	g	148		193	Á	238	î
14		59	;	104	h	149		194	Â	239	ï
15		60	<	105	i	150		195	Ã	240	ð
16		61	=	106	j	151		196	Ä	241	ñ
17		62	>	107	k	152		197	Å	242	ò
18		63	?	108	l	153		198	Æ	243	ó
19		64	@	109	m	154		199	Ç	244	ô
20		65	A	110	n	155		200	È	245	õ
21		66	B	111	o	156		201	É	246	ö
22		67	C	112	p	157		202	Ê	247	÷
23		68	D	113	q	158		203	Ë	248	ø
24		69	E	114	r	159		204	Ì	249	ù
25		70	F	115	s	160		205	Í	250	ú
26		71	G	116	t	161	¡	206	Î	251	û
27	ESC	72	H	117	u	162	¢	207	Ï	252	ü
28		73	I	118	v	163	£	208	Ð	253	ý
29		74	J	119	w	164	¤	209	Ñ	254	þ
30		75	K	120	x	165	¥	210	Ò	255	ÿ
31		76	L	121	y	166	¦	211	Ó		
32	space	77	M	122	z	167	§	212	Ô		
33	!	78	N	123	{	168	¨	213	Õ		
34	"	79	O	124	|	169	©	214	Ö		
35	#	80	P	125	}	170	ª	215	×		
36	$	81	Q	126	~	171	«	216	Ø		
37	%	82	R	127	del	172	¬	217	Ù		
38	&	83	S	128	€	173	-	218	Ú		
39	'	84	T	129		174	®	219	Û		
40	(	85	Y	130		175		220	Ü		
41	)	86	V	131		176	°	221	Ý		
42	*	87	W	132		177	±	222	Þ		
43	+	88	X	133		178	²	223	ß		
44	,	89	Y	134		179	³	224	à		
45	-	90	Z	135		180	´	225	á		

Index

Also from Payne-Gallway:

'A' Level Computing (4th Edition)

by P.M. Heathcote

April 2000   400 pp   ISBN 1 903112 21 4

This text gives comprehensive coverage f the AQA 'A' Level Computing specification, and is also suitable for other 'A' Level Computing courses. Exercises and questions from past exam papers are given at the end of each chapter.

The answers and a complete set of OHP masters are available to teachers from our web site.

Computing Projects in Visual Basic .NET

by D. Christopher

May 2003   288 pp   ISBN 1 903112 91 5

Computing Projects In Visual Basic .NET has been written mainly for students of 'AS'/'A' level Computing, 'A' level ICT and AVCE ICT. The book assumes no knowledge of programming and covers everything needed to write a large program. Students on other courses of a similar standard, such as BTEC National, and first year HND and degree courses, should also find the material useful. The OOP (Object-Oriented Programming approach) is explained and used where applicable.

Part 1 goes through all the main programming concepts. Part 2 covers a variety of topics which students will find useful in their project work. Part 3 goes through each stage in designing and coding a full project and includes a sample project.

Computing Projects in Visual Basic

by D. Christopher

September 2000   256 pp   ISBN 1 903112 33 8

This text covers similar material to Visual Basic .NET. Part 1 and the project in Part 3 can be done using Visual Basic version 4 or higher. Some topics in Part 2 require version 5 or higher.

Tackling Computer Projects in Access with Visual Basic for Applications (3rd edition)

by P.M.Heathcote

March 2000   200pp   ISBN 1 903112 22 2

This book will help students on a Computing course to complete a project in MS Access. It covers database design, creating tables, forms and subforms, queries, importing and exporting data to other packages, analysing and processing data, reports, and programming in Visual Basic for Applications. It includes advice on choice of projects and a sample project.

*See our web site **www.payne-gallway.co.uk** for latest titles and prices, and online ordering.*

Software:

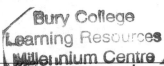

Algorithms and Data Structures (2nd edition)

by P.M.Heathcote and E.Morgan

Published March 1st 1998. Site Licence available
ISBN 0 9532490 1 8

This highly popular interactive package can be loaded and run on a network and gives students approximately 10 hours of interactive tuition on how to tackle problems involving data structures. It contains 6 units covering Programming fundamentals, Sorting and Searching, Linked Lists, Queues, Stacks and Trees. A seventh unit tests students on the concepts they have learned.

Revision Software

Content author: Alison Day   Software: A.Baillie and R.Woods

This interactive revision software is an enjoyable way of revising and stimulating class discussions on different Computing and ICT topics. The packages contain questions for the AQA modules written by experienced examiner Alison Day. Packages are supplied on CD and may be installed on any computer in the school or college. They may also be run from a server.

Each package consists of several quizzes on different areas of the specification with up to 9 different topic areas being covered in each package. A random 10 questions from a bank of 30 or more on each topic are given each time a student attempts a quiz, and a full explanation is given after each question is attempted.

'AS' Computing Revision	Published March 2002	(Upgrade due March 2004)
'A2' Computing Revision	Published January 2003	(Upgrade due March 2004)
'AS' ICT Revision	Published March 2002	(Upgrade due March 2004)
'A2' ICT Revision	Published January 2003	(Upgrade due March 2004)

Each package is available as a Lifetime site license, or as an Annual site license which will be automatically converted to Lifetime after 2 years. Upgrades will be available at a reduced price to holders of a Lifetime site licence. Single-user licenses may also be purchased.
Consult our web site www.payne-gallway.co.uk for details.

Hundreds of centres have already discovered the benefits of these computer-aided learning packages, written especially for 'A' Level Computing and ICTstudents and unique in the market! The packages are straightforward to install and run, offer excellent value for money and keep students interested and motivated.

The software is supplied on CD-ROM for Windows 95, 98, NT Server, 2000 or XP (but not MacOS). Inspection copies of books and a free demo disk of 'Algorithms and Data Structures', 'ICT Revision' and 'Computing Revision' are available to teachers from our distributors:

BEBC Distribution
P.O. Box 3371
Poole, Dorset
BH12 3YW
Tel: 01202 712909   Fax: 01202 712913   E-mail: pg@bebc.co.uk